In
U1
Monetary Policy

Inflation, Unemployment, and Monetary Policy

Robert M. Solow and
John B. Taylor

The Alvin Hansen
Symposium on
Public Policy
Harvard University

*edited and with an
introduction by
Benjamin M. Friedman*

The MIT Press
Cambridge, Massachusetts
London, England

First MIT Press paperback edition, 1999

This book was set in Palatino by Achorn Graphic Services and was printed and bound in the United States of America.

Library of Congress Cataloging-in-Publication Data

Alvin Hansen Symposium on Public Policy (1st: 1995: Harvard University)
   Inflation, unemployment, and monetary policy / Robert M. Solow and John B. Taylor ; edited and with an introduction by Benjamin M. Friedman.
      p.   cm.
   Papers and discussion presented at the First Alvin Hansen Symposium on Public Policy, held at Harvard University on April 24, 1995.
   Includes bibliographical references and index.
   ISBN 0-262-19397-3 (hc : alk. paper), 0-262-69222-8 (pb)
   1. Monetary policy—United States—Congresses. 2. Inflation (Finance)—United States—Congresses. 3. Unemployment—United States—Congresses. 4. Board of Governors of the Federal Reserve System (U.S.) I. Solow, Robert M. II. Taylor, John B. III. Title.
HG540.A37   1995
332.4'973—dc21   97-14979
                                                                        CIP

Contents

Introduction   vii
Benjamin M. Friedman

1 How Cautious Must the Fed Be?   1
Robert M. Solow

2 Monetary Policy Guidelines for Employment and Inflation Stability   29
John B. Taylor

3 Comments   55
Benjamin M. Friedman
James K. Galbraith
N. Gregory Mankiw
William Poole

4 Responses   89
Robert M. Solow
John B. Taylor

5 Rejoinder 103

John B. Taylor
Robert M. Solow

Contributors 107
Notes 109
References 111
Index 115

Introduction

Benjamin M. Friedman

The connection between price inflation and real economic activity has been a central focus of interest to macroeconomists for much of the last century. It has likewise been a, if not *the*, central issue in the making of monetary policy. Moreover, opinion among both economists and policymakers has swung widely over the years on even the most basic questions concerning how economies actually behave in this regard, and therefore on just what monetary policy can and should do.

As of today, practically everyone interested in the conduct of monetary policy acknowledges that central bank actions can and often do affect both inflation and measures of real economic activity like output, employment, and incomes. Modern macroeconomics has established familiar sets of conditions under which this would not be so—that is, conditions under which monetary policy would influence prices while leaving aggregate real activity unchanged—but to state these conditions and understand just how they would render monetary policy neutral in this sense is different from believing that they actually obtain in any known economy. As a result, the tension created by the joint effect of central bank actions on inflation *and* on aggregate output, or employment, is usually of the essence whenever public policy discussion turns to monetary policy.

Merely to say that monetary policy affects both inflation and real economic outcomes, however, is to ignore the subtlety of the matter as well as to understate the difficulty of the resulting set of problems confronting monetary policymakers. The two-way interaction between monetary policy and economic behavior is a process that operates over time. Some consequences of central bank actions occur before others. Some are permanent, others only transitory. And some may be transitory yet sufficiently long-lasting that in the eyes of policymakers and the public (not to mention researchers who try to infer such distinctions on the basis of empirical evidence), for all practical purposes they might just as well be permanent. These complex and imperfectly understood dynamics present particular difficulties for monetary policymakers, whose responsibility it is in a democratic system to reflect public views of the public good.

A key reason for the continual evolution of opinion on how policymakers should resolve these and other related tensions is the difficulty of establishing with any precision how the world that is relevant to monetary policymaking actually works. Macroeconomics is not a laboratory science. The basis for distinguishing among competing hypotheses is not replicated experimentation, but inference from limited actual experience that normally represents anything but a controlled experiment. Hence the same observed behavior of the economy—the same recessions, the same inflations, the same economic responses to not only central bank actions but also fiscal changes and asset price movements and exchange rate variations and oil price shocks and countless other events, all happening at once—is subject to sometimes widely differing interpretations. And, moreover, objective aspects of the economic environment also change. Even if economists at some time could give policymakers a satisfactorily accurate description of how specific central bank actions affected inflation and real activity, changes over time in the composition of industry, in the structure of the financial markets, in the economy's openness to flows of goods and assets, in government regulation, and in everyday business practice would soon render that description out of date.

The papers presented by Robert Solow and John Taylor at the first Alvin Hansen Symposium on Public Policy address the practical dilemma currently confronting American monetary policy. Inflation has slowed from the rapid pace that aroused such intense public dismay a decade and a half ago. Economic expansion since the last recession ended has been persistent though hardly vigorous. Both employment and unemployment have reached levels that in the past have often caused prices to accelerate. In these circumstances policymakers face opportunities as well as risks, and the uncertainties—not only on specifics but also about more fundamental aspects of how the economy behaves and how monetary policy affects that behavior—are, as always, large. How, then, should the Federal Reserve System proceed? The objective of these papers and the discussion that follows is to make a practical contribution to resolving this important public policy question.

Acknowledgments

The papers and discussion published here were presented
at the first Alvin Hansen Symposium on Public Policy,
held at Harvard University on April 24, 1995. In introduc-
ing these proceedings, I want to express my very sincere
personal thanks, as well as the gratitude of the Harvard
Economics Department, to Marian Hansen Merrifield and
Leroy Sorenson Merrifield. Their generosity has made possible not only this first Alvin Hansen Symposium but also the
entire series of public policy symposia that the Economics
Department will now sponsor at Harvard in Alvin Hansen's
name. I have enjoyed enormously working with Marian and
Leroy throughout the process of establishing this symposium series. I admire both their generosity and their sense
of public purpose.

Numerous former students of Alvin Hansen also contributed to making this symposium series possible, and on be-
half of the Harvard Economics Department I thank them as
well. Their eager participation in this effort stands as testimony to the profound and positive effect that Professor
Hansen had on so many younger economists.

I am also grateful to James Duesenberry and Richard
Musgrave, who served with me on the organizing committee that established the Alvin Hansen Symposium series and
then arranged the content of this first symposium; to Helen
Deas, who did a prodigious amount of work in arranging
the symposium's logistics; to Terry Vaughn of the MIT
Press, for his support in bringing these proceedings to publi-
cation; and especially to Robert Solow and John Taylor, as

well as my three fellow discussants, for contributing their papers and comments.

In 1967 Alvin Hansen, then in his 80th year, received the American Economic Association's Francis E. Walker medal. James Tobin, in presenting this award, described him as follows:

Alvin H. Hansen, a gentle revolutionary who has lived to see his cause triumphant and his heresies orthodox, an untiring scholar whose example and influence have fruitfully changed the directions of his science, a political economist who has reformed policies and institutions in his own country and elsewhere without any power save the force of his ideas. From his boyhood on the South Dakota prairie, Alvin Hansen has believed that knowledge can improve the condition of man. In the integrity of that faith he has had the courage never to close his mind and to seek and speak the truth wherever it might lead. But Professor Hansen is to be honored with as much affection as respect. Generation after generation, students have left his seminar and his study not only enlightened but also inspired—inspired with some of his enthusiastic conviction that economics is a science for the service of mankind.

Inflation, Unemployment, and Monetary Policy

1   How Cautious Must the Fed Be?

Robert M. Solow

Since this is the first Hansen Symposium and since none of us is getting any younger, I would like to begin with a few words about Alvin Hansen's approach to the problem of inflation. My purpose is not to trace the evolution of his thought, but to make a point. I take as my text the first 40 pages of *Economic Issues of the 1960s,* four short chapters on "The Inflation Debate" of the time. Hansen was then 75 years old, so we may safely take this discussion as his mature attitude. There is a lot in it that I find sensible and attractive.

For those who were not yet born in 1960, or whose grade-school curriculum was light on discussion of inflation, I should describe the episode that was in Hansen's—and the profession's—mind. The source of concern was the fact that the Consumer Price Index rose at an average rate of 2.4 percent per year during the routine business-cycle upswing from 1955 to 1957, and then by another 2.8 percent in the *recession* year, 1958. It was the failure of the price level to fall in the recession that elicited anguished discussion of this new sort of "creeping inflation." It all seems a little quaint, but only the facts, not the ideas.

Hansen reviews the then-current vocabulary of "demand-pull" and "wage-push" as sources of inflation, but he is not at all inclined to be doctrinaire. He looks at each little episode of rising price-level in the postwar period. For 1955–1957 he adopts the view first put forward by Charles Schultze. There was clearly a strong investment boom. The very sharp rise in the associated prices—producer durables, metals and metal products, industrial construction—is no mystery; there was excess demand. For the general price level to be constant, other prices would have to be falling on the average. Hansen shows that there was no excess demand outside of the investment sector. But costs were pulled up by events in the durable-goods industry; and higher costs worked against price reductions and, in some instances, got translated into small price increases. The "ratchet effect" that kept prices from falling in the recession of 1958 is attributed to "administered prices" or, as we might say, "downward stickiness."

One short chapter is devoted to a demonstration that the events of 1955–1958 were not really out of line with the course of prices in earlier twentieth-century business cycles. The moral is that public policy should not overreact. Hansen's view is that downward stickiness is likely to translate business-cycle fluctuations into a rising trend of prices. The right way to deal with this is to try to iron out investment fluctuations. He suggests such devices as automatic countercyclical variation in income-tax rates, to reinforce built-in stabilization, and a similar countercyclical variation in rates of depreciation allowable for corporate-tax purposes. He has some good things to say for the old Swedish policy of allowing businesses to make tax-free deposits of profits into blocked investment reserves which can then be unblocked when a recession begins, allowing firms to spend them without incurring any tax liability. He also endorses some sort of incomes policy, with tripartite involvement in wage bargaining.

On the determination of output and employment, it is pretty clearly Alvin Hansen speaking. On inflation itself, the tone is gently eclectic. Hansen had come around to the view that squeezing the last percentage point or two of inflation out of the U.S. economy would require so contractionary a combination of fiscal and monetary policy that the cost in percent-years of unemployment could not be justified. He was anything but a flat-earther.

This recollection of Hansen's style suggests another preliminary comment. We are interested in the relation between the state of the real economy, usually summarized in the unemployment rate, and the presence, or imminence, or prospect of inflation. Behind that question is another: When should discretionary macroeconomic policy turn from being expansionary or neutral to being contractionary, in order to prevent or postpone inflationary pressures?

In Hansen's mind, macroeconomic policy would automatically include both fiscal and monetary policy. Today we think almost entirely in terms of monetary policy. The main reason for that is practical. The attachment of voters to public services for which they are unwilling to tax themselves has more or less paralyzed fiscal policy and made it vulnerable to lowest-common-denominator politics. Even under better conditions, discretionary fiscal policy is likely to be contentious and slow.

In addition, the financial press sometimes writes as though there is some special direct connection between the money supply and the price level. So far as fundamentals are concerned, monetary policy works through its effects on aggregate nominal demand, just like fiscal policy, in the short run and, with allocational amendments, in the long run, too. The only direct connection I can think of is itself the creation of pop economics. If business people and others become convinced that there is some causal immaculate connection from the money supply to the price level, completely bypassing the real economy, then the news of a monetary-policy action will generate inflationary or disinflationary expectations and induce the sorts of actions that will tend to bring about the expected outcome and thus confirm the expectations and strengthen the underlying beliefs.

That sort of consideration is not the subject of discussion on this occasion. For present purposes only, I am willing to identify macroeconomic policy with monetary policy. Hansen might not like it, but the pragmatist in him would go along.

That is a good note on which to turn to the question of the day. The main point I want to make is that serious discussions of unemployment and inflation could use a little more pragmatism—not to say skepticism—than they usually get. I am willing, for now, to accept the broad outline of the standard doctrine on the subject. (I will specify in a minute what I mean by that.) But I want to argue that those who accept it should accept it with rather less confidence than they seem to exhibit and should acknowledge more uncertainty about the values of the key parameters, and even about their stability, than now seems to be the fashion. The most radical thing I want to suggest is that monetary policy could afford to go in for a trial-and-error approach to finding a fair balance between the dangers of inflation and the benefits of high output and employment.

The standard doctrine is the sort of model usually described as "accelerationist." That means: there is a degree of supply-demand balance in the economy as a whole, usually measured by the unemployment rate although the rate of capacity utilization and the vacancy rate seem to work just as well, with the property that inflation speeds up if the economy is tighter and decelerates if the economy is slacker. That special state of the real economy is usually called the "natural rate" of unemployment, or the NAIRU. I like neither term, the first because it intends deliberately to claim more for that state of the economy than anyone has ever seriously argued it deserves, and the second because it is terrible English. I could sit still for "equilibrium rate," but that choice of words begs the question of the nature of the underlying equilibrium mechanism. I will settle for calling it the neutral rate of unemployment, not that it matters.

Anyway, there is pretty convincing evidence that the U.S. economy, since about 1970, has behaved in a way consistent with the accelerationist model. I do not think that could be said of the United States before 1970, nor is it so clear for much of Europe today. That shadow of impermanence is a relevant part of the case I will be making as I go along.

The neutral unemployment rate defined by a standard accelerationist model does not have to be constant in time. Other sources of inflationary pressure help to determine the current neutral rate. The usual suspects include the demographic composition of the labor force, exogenously caused increases in food and energy prices, similar impulses from import prices, imposition or removal of formal or informal price controls, and still others. It takes more slack to keep inflation from accelerating when these external impulses are strong than when they are weak. The neutral rate might also respond to occasional well-defined changes in the environment of the labor market—like the scope, duration, and generosity of unemployment insurance benefits; the strength and aggressiveness of trade unions; the presence or absence of restrictions on layoffs by employers—or to characteristics of product markets, like the intensity of international and domestic competition, though this possibility is usually neglected. What the model cannot tolerate is the need to postulate fairly frequent, spontaneous, and unexplained changes in the neutral rate itself. In those circumstances the model might be said to "work," in the sense that it can always rationalize the facts. But it would have very little predictive power, and it would be almost vacuous as a theory of inflation. (This kind of failure of the accelerationist model is not good news or bad news; it is just news.)

If the accelerationist model were true, and if the neutral rate were known with certainty, then the proper prescription for monetary policy would be pretty clear. The central bank should try to keep the real economy from straying any significant distance from the neutral rate for any significant length of time. I put it in that vague way to emphasize that there is no implicit claim that monetary policy can control the state of the real economy very precisely.

The important implication is that, even if the current rate of inflation is tolerable, there is no case for deliberately pushing the unemployment rate below the neutral rate. If it were held there forever, the result would be faster and faster inflation, and that would not be a desirable state of affairs because very fast inflation seems to be universally disliked. A temporary lowering of the unemployment rate, followed by a return to the neutral rate, would bring only a temporary increase in output. Some small part of this increment might be made permanent if it were mainly directed into productive investment. The cost would be a permanent, though limited, increase in the rate of inflation.

Even that sort of maneuver is hard to justify. Standard rules of thumb suggest that the permanent gain would be very small; and there is no good justification for inflicting higher inflation on the whole future in order to buy a temporary increment of consumption for one particular cohort of the ongoing population. According to the model, a return to the initial rate of inflation would require a roughly symmetric episode of higher-than-neutral unemployment. So the whole maneuver would amount to a shifting of unemployment and inflation from one cohort to another, with no net gain.

Just to be clear, I should point out that the injunction to keep the unemployment rate near the neutral rate is not a monetarist or automatic-pilot prescription. Keeping the economy near its neutral rate could require frequent discretionary actions from the central bank, to offset the effects of shocks to aggregate demand and, for that matter, any shocks to aggregate supply that do not change the neutral rate of unemployment.

That would more or less take care of the matter if the neutral rate were in actual fact known with certainty. That is what Robert Gordon believes, and he is the leading student of the location of the neutral rate. (He seems to have changed his mind between the time I wrote those words and the time I revised them. I allow the wording to stand, to keep the argument straightforward and to honor Gordon's open-mindedness.) Even Gordon is careful to limit this claim of precision to the United States. My next goal is to parlay the rather different experience of other countries and some bits and pieces of evidence for the United States into a counterclaim. I want to argue that there can be an economically meaningful margin of uncertainty of the whereabouts of the neutral rate at any particular time, and, even further, that it may not be the sort of stable parameter that the underlying theory needs it to be. No one should take heart at this: Reality might turn out to be worse, not better, than one used to think.

I will begin with a brief, potted version of the European story, not to be preoccupied with it, but because it is an easy way to insinuate the sort of skepticism I want to cultivate. Between 1959 and 1973, while the United States and Canada had an average unemployment rate of 4.8 percent, France got along with an unemployment rate of 2.3 percent, (West) Germany with 0.9 percent, and the United Kingdom with 2.0 percent. The whole of the European Community averaged 2.3 percent and the EFTA (European Free Trade Area) countries 1.3 percent. It may be, though it is far from a sure thing, that unemployment was then a little too low. With hindsight, it is possible to discern a slow upward drift in European unemployment beginning in the late 1960s or early '70s, but the operative word is "slow." Simple extrapolation would get nowhere near the experience of the '80s and '90s.

During the 1980s, the French unemployment rate averaged 9.6 percent, the German 7.5 percent, and the British 10 percent. The European Community average was 10.1 percent; the EFTA countries experienced higher unemployment, too, but only at 3.3 percent. The '90s have not started off looking any better and do not seem to be improving. In some countries, unemployment has been even higher. Unsurprisingly, this run-up in unemployment had a disinflationary effect. But that eventually wore off, and unemployment stagnated near 10 percent without anything that looked remotely like accelerating deflation.

The only interpretation of this experience that is consistent with the accelerationist model is that the neutral rate of unemployment must have gone from around three percent to something near 10 percent in much of Europe, no doubt a bit higher in some countries and a bit lower in others. This rather remarkable hypothesis seems to have been accepted without a qualm. (There is nothing like an adjustable, unobservable parameter to keep a theory afloat in rough seas.) The accompanying story line is that the neutral unemployment rate is so high because European labor markets are rigid and European workers immobile. Comfortable unemployment benefits allow or encourage unemployed workers to search feebly, if at all, and to turn down jobs that would require them to move or even to change occupation or industry. Other labor-market regulations reinforce the power of entrenched incumbent workers and allow them to jack up their wages without eliciting active competition for jobs from unemployed workers.

There is no doubt something to this story. European labor markets do tend to be inflexible and non-competitive; and product-market rigidities, though not often discussed, work in the same direction. But there is also an air of implausibil-

ity about it. The dramatic increase in European unemployment came, not gradually, but in a couple of big steps. In
France the unemployment rate went from four percent to
ten percent in five years and never came down. In Germany
the rise was from three percent to eight percent in only three
years. The same general picture describes some of the small
countries as well. That does not sound like the evolutionary
result of rigor mortis in the labor market. In fact, during
much of the period when unemployment was ratcheting upward, labor markets were being deregulated and social benefits reduced. Mrs. Thatcher was not alone. The process of
deregulation has continued into the '90s, but there is no sign
of the drop in the neutral rate of unemployment that should
have happened.

It used to be fashionable to explain high European unemployment by a "wage gap." Real wages were just too high
relative to productivity. This was not implausible. Real
wages in Europe did not respond as quickly to the productivity slowdown of the mid-1970s as they did in North
America. But that story does not look so good now. The
wage gap has disappeared. Profitability has been restored.
But high unemployment lingers on.

There is an alternative interpretation that makes more
sense to me. It is not an essential part of the main argument,
but I will mention it for later reference. The surges in European unemployment came as a natural result of monetary
tightening designed to squeeze out the inflation of the 1970s
and especially the surge of inflation after the second oil
shock. European central banks kept the squeeze on for a
long time. Suppose there is a tendency for prolonged "cyclical" unemployment to turn into something that looks like

"structural" unemployment. It is not hard to imagine how that might plausibly happen as the unemployed adapt to the unavailability of jobs. Then the disinflationary power of high unemployment withers away. Central banks convince themselves that they are faced with a high neutral rate and can not afford to expand aggregate demand. But it could be in fact their own tight policy that keeps the apparent neutral rate so high. (In the jargon of macroeconomics, the long-run aggregate supply curve may be vertical, but its location is endogenous to macroeconomic policy.) It would be bad news indeed if this apparently structural unemployment really would not yield to the revival of the demand for goods and labor. But the history of the United States in the 1960s and the United Kingdom in the early 1980s suggests that it would.

This interpretation now has something more than common sense and casual empiricism to support it. In a recent paper, Laurence Ball (1997) has verified the existence of a clear correlation between the increase in the estimated neutral rate between 1980 and 1990 in each of twenty OECD countries (Turkey excluded) and the extent of the disinflation achieved between 1980 and 1990 in the same countries. His preferred relation, designed to capture causality from both the demand side and the supply side, connects the change in a country's estimated neutral rate to a composite variable (decrease in inflation multiplied by duration of UI benefits) and to the (squared) length of the main disinflationary episode in that country during the decade. The implication is that (a) other things equal, a country that enforced a stronger disinflation experienced a larger increase in its apparent NAIRU, and (b) given the extent of disinflation, spreading it over a long time had the effect of increasing the NAIRU. Both of these implications are consistent with the interpretation that strong and prolonged disinflation and the accompanying experience of high and prolonged unemployment lead to adjustments—on the part of the unemployed and, probably, on the part of employers as well—that tend to make unemployment look "structural." There are stories that would reverse the direction of causality—increased NAIRU leads first to high inflation and then to strong disinflation—but Ball has a convincing empirical test that confirms the original interpretation. So some of the uncertainty about the location of the neutral rate may be a side effect of recent monetary policy itself.

The point of this quick trip to Europe is not to propose an alternative to the accelerationist model but to suggest that today's neutral rate is not exactly structural bedrock. It can change for supply-side reasons and very likely for demand-side reasons as well. If that is so, then there will be times, and they need not be exceptional, when there is uncertainty about where the neutral rate actually is. The central bank will not know, and neither will outside observers. There will be differences of opinion among serious people. The margin of doubt may not be very large; for my purposes, a percentage point or so is quite enough. In the United States today, a percentage point of unemployment corresponds to about a million and a quarter jobs and, by Okun's Law, to two percent of GDP or maybe a little more. So doubts about whether the neutral rate is 5.5 or 6.5 percent are not doubts about a matter of no importance. Resolving the doubts econometrically would be nice, but that may be asking too much.

Just to be mischievous, I once checked to see what would happen if we supposed that the neutral rate in any year was just the equally-weighted average of the unemployment rates of the past five years. Even for the United States, that model, in its crudest form, worked nearly as well as one with a constant neutral rate. For Europe, of course, it worked much better.

This model differs from the standard story in one very important way. Any unemployment rate can be the neutral rate, if only it persists long enough. Like the accelerationist model, however, it tells a pretty pessimistic story. (My alternative model allows a fairly wide range of neutral rates. But if the economy gets stuck with a high rate, the cost of moving to a lower one is a one-time, but permanent, rise in the rate of inflation.) I am not peddling optimism here; I am just casting another shadow of doubt on the stability of the neutral rate itself.

In the paper just described, Ball tries out a different independent variable: He fits a trend to each country's unemployment rate and uses the 1980–1990 increase in trend unemployment. The results are quite similar to those obtained using an explicitly estimated neutral rate, with just a slight deterioration of fit. Since a five-year trailing moving average is also a sort of trend, Ball's findings are quite consistent with my own.

A minimal guess about the appropriate degree of uncertainty can be gleaned from Gordon's own work. He is pretty confident in placing the neutral rate at 6.0 percent (for the aggregate unemployment rate). But there is internal evidence that a number as low as 5.3 percent is in the ballpark. The higher figure comes from estimation of an accelerationist Phillips curve in which there are autoregressive terms going back 24 quarters. That strikes me as implausible, but I do not want to argue about it. A set of alternative estimates, in which the lag goes back 12 quarters—a more reasonable model to my way of thinking—makes the neutral rate out to be 5.5 percent. And the use of a different price index to measure inflation offers figures as low as 5.3 percent. (It cannot be that the neutral rate for the PCE deflator is really less than that for the GDP deflator, unless you can comfortably imagine the GDP deflator engaged in accelerating inflation while the PCE deflator is acting out steady inflation.) So even on Gordon's own showing the neutral rate could be between 5.3 percent and something above six percent, which gives me the percentage-point range I mentioned earlier.

The point I am making here has now received strong confirmation from a paper by Douglas Staiger, James Stock, and Mark Watson (1997) that gives a direct and complete answer to the question: "How Precise Are Estimates of the Neutral Rate of Unemployment?" This is important enough for my purposes that I will quote at length from their Abstract. "The main finding is that the NAIRU is imprecisely estimated: A typical 95-percent confidence interval for the NAIRU in 1990 is 5.1 percent to 7.7 percent. This imprecision obtains whether the natural rate is modeled as a constant, as a slowly changing function of time, as an unobserved random walk, or as a function of various labor market fundamentals; it obtains using other series for unemployment and inflation, including additional supply shift variables in the Phillips curve, using monthly or quarterly data, and using various measures for expected inflation. This imprecision suggests caution in using the NAIRU to guide monetary policy." My eventual conclusion will differ slightly from that last sentence; but their main conclusion fits my argument like a glove.

Robert Eisner, who may be even more of a skeptic about all this than I am, has thrown another bit of uncertainty into the pot. Eisner's main finding is that the accelerationist Phillips curve appears to be a valid econometric relation only for unemployment rates above the neutral rate. In other words, the data tell him that when unemployment is above 6 percent, inflation tends to decelerate. But he finds that there is not much evidence that lower unemployment rates go with accelerating inflation. His interpretation is that the Phillips coefficient is much smaller at low unemployment rates, and he is evidently prepared to translate that belief into policy. My interpretation is that the relation just becomes mushy. When the mushiness resolves itself in each instance, it could be for better or for worse. I draw the further conclusion that mushiness is infectious. It seems unlikely that there is a sharp, reliable acceleration relation for unemployment rates above 6 percent that just happens to disappear for lower unemployment rates. Eisner's results make me see an aura of vagueness about the whole causal chain, vagueness or uncertainty rather than disbelief. I would not be inclined to build Eisner's finding into policy.

Here I should mention some analogous results of my own. I have done a little exploration with monthly, rather than quarterly, data. I admit that I was fishing for uncertainty, not belief. One of the things I did is to separate the data into three bins: One contains months following two months (or more) of accelerating inflation; a second bin con-

tains monthly observations following two months of decelerating inflation; the third bin contains all the other months.
An accelerationist Phillips curve seems to fit for months in
the first bin, but it tends to fall apart in the other two bins.
It is interesting that, in this experiment, the "good" observations are on the "strong economy" side; in Eisner's estimates
the "good" observations are on the "weak economy" side.
There are a lot of good observations in any case, and I would
not exclude the possibility that Gordon's confidence is justified. But I would say that a prudent policymaker would be
unwise to act as if he or she knew with any precision where
the natural rate actually is in today's economy.

Well, then, how should the prudent central banker behave? That is the heart of the problem, and it is directly relevant today. We all know that the Federal Reserve began
raising short-term interest rates early in 1994, when the unemployment rate was running at about 6.5 percent and inflation was clearly decelerating. Many people wondered
why. The predictable answer took two forms, not at all mu-
tually exclusive: the long-lag response and the genie-and-
the-bottle response. The first says that central banks have to
take counter-inflationary action long before inflation begins
to accelerate because monetary policy operates with a long
lag. If they wait until accelerating inflation is visibly upon
us, it is already too late because too much acceleration will
have happened before today's tightening can begin to con-
tract the real economy. Central banks have to judge rates of
change as well as levels. The second response is closely related. It says that there is something asymmetrically irreversible about accelerating inflation. By the time it has

started, the genie is out of the bottle and it is all but impossible to stuff the genie back where it belongs.

I believe that the second of these clichés is wrong and that, without it, the first response loses much of its force. The conclusion I have drawn is that central banks should admit that they do not know, to within a percentage point of unemployment, how much prosperity they can allow. That being so, they can afford to explore, to experiment, to move forward a step at a time. If they go a little too far, they can back off. There may be a genie, but there is no bottle. Central banks can reverse themselves. The cost of making an error of the second kind may not be zero, but it need not be large, and it may be small compared with the loss from running the economy a couple of percentage points short of its potential.

For evidence, I will appeal again to the work of Gordon and Eisner, supplemented by an experiment of my own. In a recent paper, after establishing to his own satisfaction that the neutral rate of unemployment is 6 percent, Gordon conducts a simulation experiment. Starting at the end of 1994, with recent history built into his lag structure, he imagines that the Fed allows (or pushes) the unemployment rate to fall to five percent by the fourth quarter of 1995, holds it there for two years until the fourth quarter of 1997, then brings it back up to 6 percent again by the fourth quarter of 1998, and holds it there until the end of 2004. Never mind that this scenario suggests a far greater capacity for fine tuning than the Fed actually has; that is not the point of the experiment. The point is to trace the effect of this real evolution on the rate of inflation.

In this application, it turns out that Gordon's long-lag and short-lag equations give very similar results. The calculated inflation rate rises sharply from 2.7 percent (per year) at the beginning of 1995 to 3.7 percent at the end of 1995 and the beginning of 1996. The short-run dynamics built into the lag structure then produces some minor fluctuations in the inflation rate, roughly between 3.5 percent and 4 percent, lasting until the end of 1999. The rate of inflation then levels off at 3.8 percent per year and stays there throughout the rest of the simulation at the end of 2004. There are three things to notice about this story. The inflation response to the lowering of the unemployment rate by one point is very prompt. Similarly, the return to the neutral rate cuts off the tendency for inflation to increase with little or no delay. The overall response is fairly sluggish. The fact that the episode ends with a permanent increase in inflation from 2.7 to 3.8 percent per year is, of course, an inevitable characteristic of the accelerationist model. But there is plenty of time for the central bank to observe what is happening and to reverse itself if necessary before anything drastic happens on the inflation front.

Eisner performs a similar simulation experiment. His estimated equation is different from Gordon's; he follows the Congressional Budget Office in the details, but they are clearly members of the same somewhat extended family of accelerationist Phillips curves. Eisner uses the unemployment rate for married males instead of the more aggregate figure. His neutral rate is 3.55 percent, which would translate into 5.8 percent, or maybe even the canonical 6.0 percent, for the total unemployment rate.

He starts his simulations in the fourth quarter of 1994 and computes four alternative paths. In one of them, the unemployment rate goes at once to 3.55 percent and stays there. In the second, the unemployment rate for married males falls to 2.55 percent in the fourth quarter of 1994 and then returns in the next quarter to the neutral rate. In the third, unemployment remains at 2.55 percent for four quarters, through the third quarter of 1995, before returning to the neutral rate. In the fourth simulation, the unemployment rate stays at 2.55 percent through the end of the simulation in the fourth quarter of 1999.

The stories are a lot like Gordon's. In the first simulation, which stays at the neutral rate, the model's slightly checkered past produces some short-run dynamics, but they are over by the end of 1994 and the inflation rate (for the GDP implicit deflator) levels off at 2.2 percent per year. Even the one-quarter jolt of low unemployment produces more drastic dynamics. The inflation rate goes as high as 3.8 percent for one quarter and as low as 1.6 percent for a couple of quarters. But it is all over by the end of 1995, and inflation levels off at 2.3 percent per year, almost indistinguishable from the first run. The third simulation, with a low unemployment rate for a whole year, is of course more drastic. The inflation rate fluctuates until the end of 1996 and then levels off at 2.8 percent annually. The last simulation must yield accelerating inflation. Even then, the impression of sluggishness remains. Inflation does not reach five percent annually until early in 1999. That is not a tolerable outcome; the point is that the simulation takes four years to produce an increase in inflation of 2.5 percent.

Once again, there is no trace of a genie in a bottle. The overwhelming impression is of continuity, even sluggishness. A central bank that was groping around to find the bottom of the range of safe unemployment rates would apparently know pretty quickly when it had gone too far. It could afford to reverse course and pull back a bit. Even if the monetary-policy lag itself were reasonably long, there is no cliff to fall off, no sudden irreversible take-off. One might guess that, if the central bank were open about what it is doing, as the Fed—prodded by Alan Blinder— has recently been, the policy lag would not be very long either. The models I have described do not fish for irreversibility, so they do not find it. But I am not aware of anyone who has fished and caught something.

I want to dwell longer on this point because it is often the occasion for careless reasoning. The possibility that there are long lags in the transmission mechanism is a legitimate reason for caution in pushing and changing monetary policy. The intended effects may arrive only after circumstances have changed, and the results may be perverse. Even if that sort of scenario is unlikely, as it probably is, there is surely a better chance for quantitative error in proportioning policy to need. So lags matter.

But they matter symmetrically, as far as the evidence goes. Of course a central bank that countenances too much effective demand for too long runs the risk of feeding inflation down the road, when it may regret its past actions. Inflation may get too high and stay high too long. But a central bank that turns contractionary too soon runs a symmetrical risk. It may find that it is contributing to economic weakness down the road, when it may regret its past actions. Production may get too low and unemployment too high and may stay that way too long. Those risks cannot be avoided when the control of policy over events is imprecise, and operates with a long lag. But the risk cuts both ways.

And that appears to be the story. Long policy lags are part of the folklore, and the folklore may be right. There is more to think about than just the mechanics of policy. In a recent issue of the *New England Economic Review*, Jeffrey Fuhrer emphasizes the persistency of inflation, and shows how it makes disinflation costly, in the sense that the "sacrifice ratio"—the percentage shortfall of output below potential required to reduce the inflation rate by one point—is four to six times higher than it would be if there were little or no persistence. That characteristic is independent of policy. It has to do with wage-setting and price-setting institutions, or with the formation of expectations, or perhaps with other things. What matters is that disinflation takes a long time, during which aggregate output has to be below its neutral level. One might conclude that disinflation should begin early. But everything in Fuhrer's paper is linear and works in reverse just as well. If disinflation begins too soon, output will fall below normal too soon and too far. The work that has been done on this sort of problem makes no claim for irreversibility in one direction or the other.

As hinted earlier, I have tried a few experiments along this line myself, to see if there are systematic differences in the dynamics when inflation is speeding up and when inflation is slowing down. Because the time series of inflation rates is irregular, there is a decision to be made about the criteria for accelerating or decelerating inflation. I tried a few commonsensical definitions; for example, a month of accelerating inflation occurs if the rate of inflation last month was "distinctly" higher than it was "several" months ago. Deceleration is defined similarly, and many months fall into a neutral zone. None of these experiments was able to find the sort of pattern that would lead one to believe that the switch from accelerating to decelerating inflation is harder to bring about than the reverse. One could keep trying, but it is not believable that the data are dying to say anything significant on that question.

Since there is no demonstrated asymmetry in the dynamics, an asymmetry in policy can arise only from the loss function. In the nature of the case that cannot be "demonstrated." It has not been seriously argued either; a careful argument might show that a little too much slack is more costly than a little too much inflation, but I do not want to make that claim now. My point is different, though powerful. Lags may be long, but responses are sluggish and approximately symmetric. As long as there is uncertainty about the current neutral rate of unemployment—and there is—monetary policy can afford to be exploratory. Part of its job is to feel its way to the neutral rate of unemployment, slowly and unsurely. The large body of work on these issues does not support the various popular metaphors of sudden catastrophe and subsequent irreversibility: the slippery slope, the yawning cliff, the genie that has escaped from the bottle. Pending a more careful and convincing appraisal of the loss function, the goal of monetary policy ought to be to make approximately symmetrical errors. That is harder than a more one-sided approach, but whoever said that macroeconomic policy would be easy?

It is amusing that the "genie in the bottle" metaphor is exactly the opposite of the old "pushing on a string" metaphor. Then it was believed that the central bank could easily bring an expansion to a halt but would find it difficult or impossible to get one going. Now the casual belief is that a central bank can all too easily start or sustain an expansion but would be unable to bring it to a halt promptly. Easy come, easy go.

My own small-scale research on these questions does not lead to different conclusions. I have experimented with monthly data, as much for variety as for any other reason. My instinct in these matters is minimalist. I have generally limited myself to 12-month lag distributions, on past inflation and on unemployment, because going further did not seem to change the picture significantly. For the same reason, I prefer to omit the extra causal variables and stick to lagged inflation (or acceleration) and lagged unemployment. The extra variables are plausible enough, but they smack a little of data-mining to me, and one has to respect one's allergies. My suspicion of long lags is supported by the research of Staiger, Stock, and Watson mentioned earlier. They find that lags longer than a year or so add little to Phillips-curve analysis, and, taken jointly, they produce unimpressive F-statistics. I cannot see what intuition would make one want to override that finding.

With these self-imposed limitations, my interest has been in the impulse-response function: How sensitively does future inflation respond when the unemployment rate dips below or rises above its neutral level? I would summarize the findings in two statements. The first is that the neutral rate is not very precisely defined. I am willing to start with

Gordon's 6 percent, not because the data cry out for it but because I do not want to argue about it. It should be clear that, for my purposes, it is enough that some skepticism is in order. A case could be made for a lower number, or a higher one.

The second statement does not differ substantially from the conclusion reached by Gordon and by Eisner. A shock to the unemployment rate sets off some short-run oscillations of the rate of inflation, but they happen soon, they are over quickly, and their range is very narrow, at most a couple of tenths of a percentage point on either side. Once those fluctuations have damped themselves out, as they seem to do, the enduring response of the inflation rate is modest and sluggish. It does not get out of hand. If overshoots and undershoots have to be reversed, that will take time, of course, but no more than time. During that time, nothing dramatic seems to happen. Of course, it would be better to hit the bull's eye every time.

This is not the sort of exposition that calls for a full discussion of the monthly model and a large display of simulation results. Just to have something to look at, however, I will reproduce one simulation. The underlying model is simply a monthly version of a standard accelerationist Phillips curve, involving the CPI and the unemployment rate, each with 12 months' worth of lags. The model is constrained to have a NAIRU of 6 percent. The diagram traces the path of the cumulated change in the rate of inflation if the model is perturbed in the following way. It starts with a constant rate of inflation, at 6 percent unemployment. The unemployment rate then moves gradually down to 5 percent in the course of a year, stays at 5 percent for another year, and

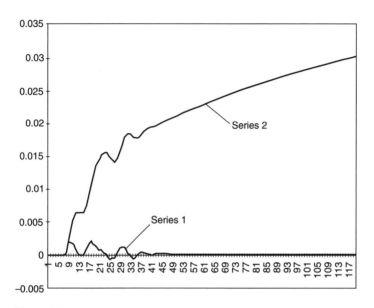

Figure 1.1
Result of a simulation: Upper curve gives cumulative change of inflation
rate from initial value; lower curve shows month-to-month changes in simulated inflation rate

then retraces its steps back to 6 percent in the course of yet
another year. The lower curve shows the month-to-month
changes in the rate of inflation; the upper curve cumulates
them from the beginning of the experiment. The second
panel of the diagram magnifies the acceleration series from
the first panel; irregular as they are, month-to-month increases in inflation never get bigger than two-tenths of a
percent per month. The truly important point is that all the
action is well contained. There is no precipitous burst of
more rapid inflation, even after a fairly substantial sojourn
below the natural rate. The whole episode is over, for all

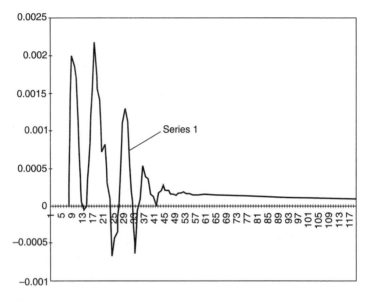

Figure 1.2
Lower curve from figure 1.1 with vertical scale magnified

practical purposes, four or five years after it began. (The continuing very slow increase is an inexactitude: The unit root in the model turned out to be 1.0027!) This is not the stuff of nightmares about runaway inflation.

These ideas have direct application to the situation to-day. The unemployment rate has been below Gordon's six-percent figure for a year or so. The most recent readings have been at 5.4 and 5.5 percent. During that time the Employment Cost Index has shown no tendency to accelerate; if anything, it has gone the other way. That does not mean we are out of the woods. Acceleration may be just around the corner, as some of my friends have been saying for more than a year. There was a chance that they would be right then, and there is a chance that they will be right now. But it is not a sure thing.

(That paragraph was written in March 1995. In June 1997, there was no reason to change a word. The unemployment rate hovered in the 5.5 to 5.7 percent range for a year, and had then slid to the neighborhood of 5.0 percent. The Employment Cost Index was neither accelerating nor decelerating, to the naked eye. Wages had speeded up a little, offset by slow growth of benefits. The odds against 6.0 or 6.5 percent being the magic number had lengthened considerably. Is the neutral rate now near 5.0 or 5.5 percent? I am really promoting skepticism that a well-defined magic number exists at all.)

Evidence for some kind of a sea-change comes from the Beveridge Curve, a plot of the unemployment rate against the job-vacancy rate (proxied by a normalized index of help-wanted advertising). James Medoff and Andrew Harless have called attention to a clear pattern in the data. A well-defined Beveridge curve in the late '50s and the '60s appears to have shifted adversely in the decade from 1975 to 1985. The shift was large: The unemployment rate associated with any given help-wanted index was two to three points higher than it had been. The data look very much as if, beginning around 1987, the Beveridge curve shifted back again until, in the 1990s, it is close to where it was in the '60s. Almost certainly, these shifts must have been accompanied by changes in the neutral unemployment rate, higher from 1975 to 1985 and lower now.

There are, after all, plausible reasons why the neutral rate *might* have drifted lower. International competition is tough;

workers and employers fear that jobs and business lost now may never be regained. The political atmosphere does not favor workers. Service industries are growing in importance, and they are not organized in exactly the same way as traditional industries. Anyone can think of other reasons. There is no way to find out without testing, and the only test-bed we have is reality itself. In the end, we have no choice but to experiment. In fact, that is exactly what we are doing—and pretty successfully, for the moment. Cautious experimentation is the *right* way to deal with parameter uncertainty, as William Brainard showed long ago.

2   Monetary Policy Guidelines for Employment and Inflation Stability

John B. Taylor

We have learned much about the unemployment-inflation trade-off and about monetary policy during the last 25 years. Both economic research—especially the research surrounding the rational expectations revolution of the 1970s—and historical experience—in particular, the inflation and disinflation of the 1970s and 1980s—have contributed to this improved understanding. In my view the change in thinking is of the same magnitude as that associated with the research surrounding the Keynesian revolution and the historical experience with the Great Depression of the 1930s. I would summarize the conclusions of the recent research and historical experience as follows.

First, there is substantial theoretical support and empirical evidence demonstrating that there is no long-run trade-off between the level of inflation and the level of unused resources in the economy—whether measured by the unemployment rate, the capacity utilization rate, or the deviation of real GDP from potential GDP.[1] Monetary policy is thus neutral in the long run: An increase in money growth will have no long-run impact on the unemployment rate; it will only result in an increase in the inflation rate. The average level of unemployment—or the natural rate—is not a constant, however; it can be affected by government policies, but these are microeconomic rather than monetary in nature.

Second, there is also substantial theoretical support and empirical evidence of short-run monetary non-neutrality. There is disagreement about the reasons for this non-neutrality or whether it even presents a trade-off to monetary policymakers. In my view it has important policy implications. It implies that monetary policies which keep aggregate demand stable have dual benefits, keeping both inflation volatility and output volatility low. But it also implies that there is a variability trade-off between the fluctuations of inflation and the fluctuations of real GDP about its growth path in the long run. That is, if both inflation stability and employment stability are the two main goals of monetary policy, there will sometimes be a choice about how much emphasis to place on one versus the other. Empirical estimates of this variability trade-off—though still preliminary—indicate that it has an important property: when inflation stability is about equal in magnitude to real GDP stability (in a sense which I will define explicitly), the trade-off becomes very steep in either direction. In other words, opportunity costs increase at a rapid rate.

Third, a general implication of research on credibility, time inconsistency, and rational expectations is that monetary policy should be viewed and conducted as much as possible as a contingency plan, or a policy rule. This research adds to earlier arguments, such as accountability and uncertainty, in favor of policy rules.

Fourth, although there is still much ongoing research on the most appropriate type of monetary policy rule to use in practice, progress has been made in determining the broad characteristics of a good monetary policy rule. I interpret recent monetary decisions in a number of countries as being roughly approximated by such a rule. However, we still need to examine the robustness of such rules to uncertainties about the real rate of interest, the natural rate of unemployment, the growth rate of potential GDP, and even the short-run trade-off between inflation and unemployment.

1 The "No Long-run Trade-off" View

Theoretical and empirical research on the relationship between inflation and unemployment has left little doubt that there is no long-run trade-off between the rate of inflation and the rate of unemployment. In other words, the unemployment rate will average about the same amount, whether the average inflation rate is zero percent or, say, ten percent. Milton Friedman and Edmund Phelps provided the theoretical underpinnings for this view nearly 30 years ago. Phelps and Friedman argued that if everyone correctly anticipated that inflation would be ten percent per year, then people would adjust their wage contracts and price increases accordingly; real wages and relative prices—and thus real variables like the unemployment rate—would be exactly what they would be with a zero inflation rate. Thus a monetary policy which brought about a higher inflation would not bring about a lower unemployment rate: Eventually people would come to expect the higher inflation rate, and the unemployment rate would remain at a level that has come to be called the natural unemployment rate.

To see what the "no long-run trade-off" view means empirically, consider the following unemployment and inflation data for the United States for four decades:

	Unemployment Rate (Civilian)	Inflation Rate (CPI)
1963	5.7	1.6
1972	5.6	3.4
1978	6.1	9.0
1987	6.2	4.4
1994	6.1	2.7

For each of these years the unemployment rate was in the neighborhood of 6 percent. But observe the large differences in the inflation rate. Inflation rose from the 1960s through the late 1970s and then began to decline again. The table shows that regardless of whether the inflation rate was low, as in the early 1960s and early 1990s, or high as in the 1970s, the unemployment rate was about the same value. In other words, when viewed over longer periods, higher rates of inflation do not bring forth lower levels of unemployment; nor do lower levels of inflation bring forth higher levels of unemployment.

I have purposely chosen these years as examples showing the economy in about the same phase of the business cycle; each year was during an economic expansion when real GDP was about equal to potential GDP. The results would be the same if one presented the data in different ways, such as averages over each of the four decades.

The experience with inflation and unemployment during the 1970s illustrated in the above table was not confined to the United States (Taylor 1992). Inflation rose in Canada, most of Western Europe, and in many of the Pacific basin countries. The inflation was a persistent, worldwide phenomenon. Yet there was no tendency for the unemployment rate to fall in any of these countries during this period. In my view, the experience with the great inflation of the 1970s and subsequent great disinflation of the 1980s provides lessons about the impact of an inflationary monetary policy. These lessons complement the lessons about the impact of a deflationary monetary policy from the devastating Great Depression of the 1930s when unemployment rose to more than 25 percent in the United States.

Deflation

To be sure, the recent experience in the table does not include any years with negative inflation, or even with zero inflation, though the 1.6 percent rate in the early 1960s could approximate zero if the upward bias in measuring inflation is of that magnitude. One of the reasons why very low levels of inflation might bring about higher average unemployment is that—with the nominal interest rate bounded below by zero—the real interest rate might not be able to fall low enough to avoid a prolonged recession or a very slow recovery from a recession.

A useful recent addition to research on this important issue has been put together by Fuhrer and Madigan (1994), who simulated an estimated rational expectations model with a zero inflation target; they found that if the central bank followed a feedback rule for monetary policy there is very little deterioration of macroeconomic stability, even with a zero inflation target. However, targeting a negative inflation rate could cause problems. There are few historical periods with persistent negative inflation (deflation) during which unemployment has not been high. One possible exception is the late nineteenth century in the United States, when the price level fell gradually and real growth was high.

Recent Revisionism

Recently some economists have questioned the modern view that there is a long-run trade-off, harking back to "Phillips Curve" views common in the early 1960s in the United States (see Eisner 1995 and Fair 1996). Fair reports on regression results from thirty countries using data from the past three decades, showing statistics that disprove the hypothesis that there is no long-run trade-off. Although the estimated regression equations, involving many variables and lags, are quite complex, the main reason for the rejection centers on the role of the previous periods' inflation rate—a proxy for expectations of inflation and slow price adjustment—in an equation explaining the current inflation rate. If inflation in previous periods affects current inflation any less than "point for point," then he concludes that there is a long-run trade-off. For example, using his estimated regressions he calculates that an expansionary monetary policy which lowers the unemployment rate by 1 percent permanently will have no long-run impact on the inflation rate.

Statistical tests of this kind were used in the 1960s to examine the trade-off. However, the tests were criticized effectively by Sargent (1971), who showed that there is no necessary relationship between the "point-for-point" hypothesis (sometimes called the "alpha equals one" hypothesis) and the non-existence of a trade-off. For example, if inflation is low and stable as it was over much of the period Phillips estimated his original equations, then one would suspect the extrapolation coefficient on lagged inflation to be low because people's expectation would be that an increase in inflation would be temporary. Sargent's (1971) critique was at the heart of the rational expectations revolution, and it applies to more recent findings. In fact, as the experience with low inflation in many countries lengthens (we have already had nearly fifteen years of observations with lower, more stable inflation), it is likely that the estimated regression coefficient on lagged inflation will gradually get smaller and smaller. As it does, Sargent's critique will be more and more relevant.

Changes in the Natural Rate

It is important to emphasize that the lack of a long-run relationship between the unemployment rate and the inflation rate does not mean that the natural rate of unemployment is a constant. Indeed, the dramatic rise in unemployment in Europe, compared with that of the United States, since the 1980s is most likely because of a rise in the natural unemployment rate in Europe. Lindbeck (1993) and Phelps (1994) review the determinants of the natural rate of unemployment, including search theories, efficiency wage theories, and insider–outsider theories, and use these theories to analyze the reasons for the rise in unemployment in Europe.

The greater flexibility of labor markets in the United States compared with Europe partly explains the lower unemployment rate in the United States, but large differences in unemployment within individual European countries indicate that there are still great uncertainties about the microeconomic determinants of the natural unemployment rate.

Economic Growth Effects

It also should be emphasized that there is now empirical evidence of another aspect of the relationship between real variables and inflation. Recent cross-sectional studies by Fischer (1993) and Motley (1994) show that countries with higher rates of inflation tend to have a lower long-term growth rate for potential GDP. Thus, even though inflation does not affect the average capacity utilization rate or unemployment rate it does appear to be correlated with the growth of productivity or income per capita. Much of the variation behind this correlation is for high inflation rates, and the evidence does not provide much information on the effects of changes in inflation in the range of 0–3 percent.

As with any correlation, one can debate the reasons for the correlation between inflation and productivity growth. One view is that the uncertainty caused by high rates of inflation may interfere with the efficient allocation of resources thereby reducing productivity growth. In any case the empirical findings give one an additional reason to be concerned—and to be added to the usual welfare costs of inflation calculations—that high rates of inflation may reduce economic efficiency.

2   The Short-run and the Output-Inflation Variability Trade-off

If there is no long-run trade-off between inflation and unemployment, then what kind of trade-off is there? Most monetary theories of the business cycle imply that there is a short-term trade-off in the sense that *changes* in inflation are associated with the level of the unemployment rate. In particular, the inflation rate tends to fall when unemployment is above the natural rate, or real GDP is below potential GDP, and inflation tends to rise when unemployment is below the natural rate, or real GDP is above potential GDP. There is strong empirical evidence for this kind of correlation in many countries: Technically, real GDP tends to Granger-cause inflation positively (see Taylor 1992).

However, I have found this short-run relationship between inflation and unemployment to be cumbersome for the evaluation of monetary policy. Its main defect is that it focuses attention on single short-run episodes rather than on the long-term, which consists of many short-runs. This defect becomes quite relevant in the evaluation of monetary policy that focuses (as I argue below) on policy rules, or contingency plans, that are evaluated and reconsidered over the long run, rather than a single decision made at a single point in time.

A Variability Trade-off

For this reason, it is useful to construct and estimate a variability trade-off between inflation and unemployment in terms of their fluctuations over time rather than their levels

during any one episode in time. In particular, I have argued
that there is a trade-off between the size of the fluctuations
in inflation and the size of the fluctuations in real GDP, or
nearly equivalently in the size of fluctuations in the unemployment rate. (The deviations of real GDP from potential
GDP and the deviations of the unemployment rate from the
natural rate are, of course, highly correlated according to
Okun's law). This trade-off can be illustrated with a "production possibilities curve" as shown in figure 2.1. On the
horizontal axis is a measure of real GDP stability. By definition, smaller and less persistent recessions and booms, or
smaller deviations of real GDP from potential GDP, constitute more real GDP stability (one could use the variance or
the standard deviation to measure the size of the fluctuations).[2] On the vertical axis is inflation stability. Again, by
definition, smaller and less persistent deviations of inflation
from some average, or target, level of inflation constitute
more inflation stability.

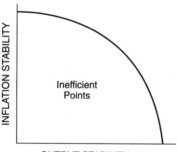

OUTPUT STABILITY

Figure 2.1
Trade-off between inflation stability and output stability

The curve is like a production possibilities curve in the sense that efficient macroeconomic policies would lead to outcomes on the curve. Points outside the curve are impossible, given existing knowledge. As long as the business cycle is not repealed and inflation is subject to unavoidable shocks, this impossible region will exist. Inefficient policies would lead to outcomes inside the curve—as with any production possibilities curve—with both inflation fluctuations and unemployment fluctuations higher than could be achieved with better policies. One can view progress in policymakers' ability to conduct macroeconomic policy—perhaps through the lessons learned about depression in the 1930s and inflation of the 1970s (both situations well within the curve)—as movements from the inefficient region toward the frontier.

But when the economy is on the frontier of the curve, one must view reduced inflation stability as the opportunity cost of better output stability. Or, equivalently, one must view reduced output stability as the opportunity cost of improved inflation stability. In fact, as with any curved production possibilities frontier, the opportunity costs are increasing: Reductions in the size of business cycle fluctuations require ever-increasing amounts of inflation instability. As I will explain later, empirical evidence suggests that the opportunity costs are *sharply* increasing.

The Theory

How does one explain the existence of such a trade-off? The economy is always subject to shocks, including *price shocks* such as a sharp, unanticipated increase in oil prices, and *aggregate demand shocks*, such as a shift in government purchases or change in demand for exports from abroad. A good macroeconomic policy will try to keep these shocks to a minimum—for example, by avoiding sharp, unanticipated shifts in monetary policy, but even in the best of circumstances such shocks are inevitable. By their very nature such shocks cause real GDP to fluctuate around what would otherwise be a smoother long-run growth path (that is, potential GDP). They also cause the inflation rate to fluctuate up and down. For example, a sharp decline in demand from abroad would cause real GDP to drop below potential GDP. An oil price shock would cause inflation to rise.

The response of monetary policy to these shocks helps determine how large the effects on real GDP or inflation will be. To see this, suppose that the economy is in a normal state where real GDP equals potential GDP and inflation is steady, and suppose that there is an upward demand shock which cannot be avoided or immediately offset by monetary policy. Once the shock occurs and causes real GDP to rise above potential GDP there will be upward pressure on the inflation rate. The monetary authorities have a choice of two responses in this circumstance: (i) If the monetary authorities tighten policy sharply in response to the rise in inflation, they will tend to reduce the pressure on inflation, but they will also tend to slow down the economy and perhaps cause a recession; or (ii) a more cautious monetary response might have less effect in taming the rise in inflation, but it will have a smaller negative effect on real GDP—perhaps a soft landing rather than a recession. The first response results in more inflation stability and less real GDP stability while the second response results in less inflation stability and more real GDP stability; hence, one begins to see the reason for a trade-off between the two measures of macroeconomic stability. The starting point for this example was a demand shock, but exactly the same type of trade-off occurs in the case of a price shock due perhaps to an oil price shock as has occurred frequently during the last twenty years. If we imagine that such shocks occur continually, we see why such a trade-off exists.

This is an intuitive explanation for the trade-off. The trade-off presents a choice to policymakers. If the policymakers have already achieved enough efficiency in policy to be on the trade-off rather than inside it (a big if), then they must choose a policy rule that takes a position on the importance of one measure of stability versus the other.

Like any production possibilities curve this output-inflation stability trade-off can shift out with improved technology. For example, better financial market data about money and credit would enable monetary policy to be made with fewer errors and thereby improve the trade-off. In addition, increases in the credibility of monetary policymakers can improve the trade-off (see Ball 1994).

The Evidence

According to this explanation, the existence of a variability trade-off is implied by the existence of a short-run trade-off between inflation and unemployment. However, is there any direct evidence?

One source of direct evidence could come from international data on a cross-section of countries. By calculating the variability of inflation and the variability of output in a cross section during a given time period, one could determine whether there was a negative correlation. The simple correlations reported by Debelle and Fischer (1994) show no such correlation. However, one would suspect that a simple correlation is insufficient evidence. Most important, there is no reason that a given cross section of countries should be on the frontier of the trade-off. Countries with an inefficient monetary policy might be well within the trade-off while countries with efficient policies would be on the trade-off. A pattern of such countries would imply a positive simple correlation coefficient. Moreover, if monetary authorities in different countries differed in their ability to control aggregate demand, there would be a positive correlation between the variability of inflation and output in a cross section. Finally, countries might have different shapes and positions for the trade-off, making a simple correlation unreliable.

Some recent work by Owyong (1996) has endeavored to deal with this problem by controlling for differences in the efficiency of central banks. Owyong uses measures of central bank independence to represent differences in the efficiency of central banks. When he controls for this variable in a regression he finds a significant negative correlation.

Estimates of the Position and the Shape of the Trade-off

Like most production possibilities curves in economics we do not know much about the exact position and shape of the output-inflation stability trade-off in figure 2.1. But estimates of the trade-off have been made by a number of researchers using estimated macroeconomic models of the economy in which different monetary policies are used. Most of these models include both rational expectations and some form of slow adjustment of wages and prices, such as a staggered wage- and price-setting framework.

The estimated trade-off depends on the model being used to estimate it, but there is an interesting and important common property of many of the estimates (see Taylor 1992). In particular, the curve appears to bend sharply near the point where the variability of real GDP fluctuations is about equal to the variability of the inflation fluctuations (that is, when the variance of the percentage deviation of real GDP from potential GDP is about equal to the variance of the inflation rate measured as an annual percentage change). In other words, the opportunity costs of more inflation stability appear to increase sharply when the fluctuations in inflation are smaller than the fluctuations in real GDP. And conversely, the opportunity costs of more output stability appear to increase sharply when the fluctuations in real GDP are smaller than the fluctuations in inflation.

This position and shape implies that the actual preferences for output stability and inflation stability do not matter much for the choice of monetary policy. In other words, as long as both macroeconomic variables are given a nonnegligible weight in society's preferences, the policy choice will involve an outcome near the relatively sharp bend in the production possibilities curve. Thus, despite the existence of this trade-off, the choice between output stability and inflation stability may not be as cruel as commonly believed. Regardless of one's preferences (excluding extremes of negligible weight on one variable), a good policy will aim for similar fluctuations in real GDP and inflation. If one plots inflation / real GDP points in a scatter diagram with inflation on the vertical axis and real GDP (measured as a deviation from potential GDP) on the horizontal axis then the scatter should look more like a circle than an ellipse. By way of comparison, the fluctuations in real GDP and inflation during the 1987–1994 cycle had real GDP fluctuating by about one percentage point more than inflation. A diagram of this would show that the scatter of points looks more like an ellipse than a circle.

3 The Rationale for Monetary Policy Rules

Modern research in macroeconomics provides many reasons why monetary policy should be evaluated and conducted as a policy rule—or contingency plan for policy—rather than as a one-time change in policy. First, the time-inconsistency literature shows that without commitment to a rule policymakers will be tempted to choose a suboptimal inflation policy—one that has a higher average inflation rate and no lower unemployment than a policy with a lower average inflation rate (see Kydland and Prescott 1977 or Barro and Gordon 1983). Second, one needs to stipulate future as well as current policy actions in order to evaluate the effects of policy. (This is a positive statement of the Lucas critique of policy evaluation.) It is why virtually all policy evaluation research on monetary policy in recent years has focused on policy rules. Third, credibility about monetary policy appears to improve its performance; sticking to a policy rule will increase credibility about future policy action. Fourth, policy rules that give market participants a way to forecast future policy decisions would reduce uncertainty. Fifth, policy rules are a way to teach new policymakers, students, and the public in general about the operations of the central bank. Finally, policy rules increase accountability, potentially requiring policymakers to account for differences between their actions and policy rules.

In arguing in favor of policy rules I recognize that certain events may require that the rule be changed or departed from; that is, some discretion is required in operating the rule. But there is still a big difference between a policy approach that places emphasis on rules and one that does not. With a policy rule in mind the analysis of policy—including questions about whether a deviation from the rule is warranted—will tend to focus more on the rule rather than pure discretion. But to be more specific about rules versus discretion one needs to be more specific about the policy rule. What should the rule be?

4 A Specific Interest Rate Rule

First consider the target inflation rate. In my view the preceding discussion implies that the central bank should choose a target for inflation and stick to it. Due to upward biases in the measure of inflation, a target of a two-percent annual inflation rate would be reasonable, and may be near an actual inflation rate of zero. With such an inflation target for monetary policy, the actual inflation rate would, of course, tend to fluctuate around 2 percent; that is, 2 percent would be the average over a period of time that would include a business cycle or longer. Currently, several central banks seem to be following policies that imply close to a two-percent target. The Bank of England, the Bank of France, and the Bundesbank are aiming for a two-percent target for inflation, so the two-percent estimate may not be far off the actual current targets.

Such an inflation target would be appropriate for any central bank. If other central banks adopted similar inflation targets, then it is likely that there would be greater stability in the international currency markets; some of the current instability of exchange rates is due to uncertainty about central bank goals for inflation.

The target for the inflation rate is not an upper bound. For example, in 1995 the inflation rate in Japan was below zero; deflation was at 2 or 3 percent. An explicit target for two-percent inflation in Japan would thereby have implied easing of Japanese monetary policy in 1995.

A more difficult question than choosing a long-run inflation target is the appropriate response of monetary policy to shocks—some of which will push the inflation rate away from its target. In general, both price shocks and aggregate demand shocks will cause real GDP to deviate from potential GDP and the inflation rate to deviate from its target. How should the central bank respond to these deviations?

A survey of simulations of econometric models with rational expectations suggests to me that monetary policy should respond in the following way (see Bryant, Hooper, and Mann 1993 for a recent tabulation of simulation results). First, the policy should respond to changes in both real GDP and inflation. Second, the policy should not try to stabilize the exchange rate, an action which frequently interferes with the domestic goals of inflation and output stability. Third, the interest rate rather than the money supply should be the key instrument that is adjusted.[3] Because of the nature of the trade-off between inflation stability and output stability, the weights on these two measures of stability appear to matter relatively little for these general conclusions.

In order to investigate the practical application of such a policy rule, several years ago I proposed a specific formula for policy that had these characteristics (see Taylor 1993). According to this policy rule the federal funds rate is increased or decreased according to what is happening to both real GDP and inflation. In particular, if real GDP rises one percent above potential GDP the federal funds rate should be raised, relative to the current inflation rate, by .5 percent. And if inflation rises by one percent above its target of 2 percent, then the federal funds rate should be raised by .5 percent relative to the inflation rate. When real GDP is equal to potential GDP and inflation is equal to its target of 2 percent, then the federal funds rate should remain at about 4 percent, which would imply a real interest rate of 2 percent on average.

The policy rule was purposely chosen to be simple. Clearly, the equal weights on inflation and the GDP gap are an approximation reflecting the finding that neither variable should be given a negligible weight.

Figure 2.2 shows how such a policy would have worked since 1987. I originally proposed this policy in November 1992, so the performance since then is in real time. According to this policy, the Fed is currently almost on course:

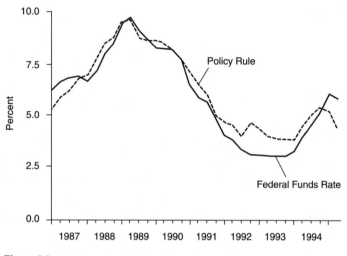

Figure 2.2
Federal funds rate, 1987–1995: actual and implied by policy rule

The federal funds rate is about 5.25 percent, about the same value given by the formula. Much of the tightening of federal reserve policy in 1994—as real GDP rose above potential and inflation began to rise—is explained by the rule.

Observe that the Fed eased in 1987 during the stock market break, representing a deviation from the policy rule, which I think made sense at the time. The only other big discrepancy was in late 1992 and 1993, when the Fed was easier than implied by the rule. There is more debate about whether that deviation was appropriate.

I originally proposed this policy rule in order to generate discussion about how such a rule could be used as a practical guideline for policy. Debates about whether deviations from the rule are appropriate or not, as well as suggestions of ways to improve the rule, are a welcome part of the discussion that has been generated thus far, and I hope debate continues. But several important concerns that have already been raised should be addressed again.

Borrowing the Good Properties of Money Supply Rules

Money supply rules have some very favorable properties. For example, they are automatically countercyclical in that when real GDP falls, the interest rate also falls, mitigating the decline in real GDP. To see this consider a k-percent money supply rule that calls for constant growth rate of the nominal money supply. In the standard demand for money equation the demand for real money balances (M/P) is a function of real income or real GDP (Y) and the short term interest rate (R). If the money supply (M) is fixed, then equilibrium in the money market implies a functional relationship between the interest rate (R), price level (P) and real GDP (Y). Along this relationship a higher level of real GDP raises the interest rate, and a higher level of inflation also raises the interest rate. Note the similarity between this relationship and the interest rate rule described above: In both cases a rise of real GDP and inflation implies that the interest rate rises. Thus, this interest rate rule has the same type of counter-cyclical features as a money supply rule. Moreover, the similarity between money supply rules and interest rate rules suggests that both have a role as a consistency check about monetary decisions.

Note also that real GDP would play a role in setting interest rates even if the central bank was entirely focused on inflation. The interest rate increase helps moderate the boom in real GDP and thereby helps stabilize both inflation as well as real GDP.

How Robust Are Interest Rate Policy Rules to Errors?

To consider some of the other issues of concern I will use some simple algebra. The policy rule described above states that:

$$i = \pi + gy + h(\pi - \pi^*) + r^{\mathrm{f}}$$

where y is real GDP measured as a percentage deviation from potential GDP; i is the short-term nominal interest rate measured in percentage points; and π is the inflation rate measured in percentage points. The parameters π^*, r^{f}, g, and h and are all positive. Thus the interest rate responds to deviation of inflation from a target π^* and to the deviations of real GDP from potential GDP. When inflation rises, the nominal interest rate rises by more than the inflation rate. When real GDP rises relative to potential GDP, the interest rate also rises. The intercept term r^{f} in this relationship is the implicit real interest rate in the central bank's reaction function. The central bank takes actions to affect the nominal interest rate by open market operations that impact the money supply. Suppose first that the long-run average value of the real GDP deviation y is 0 and let the long-run real interest rate be r^* so that in the long run $i - \pi = r^*$.

Now consider some of the things that might go wrong with the interest rate policy rule. Uncertainties about the *real interest rate* and about the level and rate of growth of *potential GDP* are likely to be great in practice. Both types of uncertainties raise problems for interest rate policy rules. To be sure, not knowing the level and growth rate of potential GDP also causes problems of most alternative approaches for the conduct of monetary policy, including money supply rules and discretion. For example, when choosing the k in the k-percent money growth rule, one needs to have an estimate of the long-run growth rate of the economy. Mistakes in the estimate of potential growth are translated into mistakes on inflation.

To consider the impact of this uncertainty, suppose that the central bank has the wrong view of the interest rate; that is, r^f does not equal r^*. Suppose also that the central bank is mistaken about the level or the growth rate of potential GDP; that is, rather than averaging the constant 0, the central bank's perceived gap variable is actually growing so that $y = a + bt$ in the long run. Plugging these values into the policy rule and solving for the equilibrium inflation rate yields $\pi = \pi^* + (r^* - r^f)/h - g(a + bt)/h$. This equation implies that if the central bank chooses a monetary policy with wrong estimates of the parameters then the steady state inflation rate π will not equal the target inflation rate π^*. If the equilibrium real interest rate r^* changes—perhaps because of a change in government spending policy—then the steady state inflation rate will change unless the central bank also adjusts its implicit real interest rate, r^f. If the parameter h is less than one, then the equation implies that there is a multiplier effect of the change in the equilibrium real interest rate on the inflation rate; that is, the inflation rate rises by more than the equilibrium real interest rate. For example, if $r^* = 3$ percent, and the Fed thinks that the real interest rate is 2 percent (that is, $r^f = 2$ percent) then the equilibrium inflation rate will be 2 percentage points above the target. A decline in the equilibrium interest rate would lead to a decline in the steady state inflation rate unless the Fed adjusts its policy.

Because the central bank does not know the equilibrium real interest rate, we cannot expect it to accurately set r^f equal to r^*, and this is a disadvantage of an interest rate policy rule compared with money growth rules. If the central bank uses an incorrect estimate of the equilibrium real interest rate, then a higher or lower inflation rate than targeted will result. However, such an error will not result in continuing increases or continuing decreases in inflation as would a policy which tries to peg the real interest rate above or below the equilibrium real interest rate. Note that the impact of the error on the long-run average inflation rate depends on the size of the response of monetary policy to the inflation rate. The larger the response parameter h, the smaller the impact of a change in the equilibrium real interest rate on the long-run average inflation rate.

Errors in estimating the level of potential GDP a cause similar problems to errors in the real interest rate. However, errors on the growth rate of potential GDP, would eventually cause inflation to perpetually rise or fall from the target. In reality, of course, the central bank would see the undesirable inflation performance and make the correction.

The Shorter Run Impacts

Many criticisms of monetary policy focus on claims that the central bank underestimates potential GDP growth. Today, for example, some feel that such an underestimation serves as a constraint on actual economic growth in the United States and that the Fed should aim for a higher growth rate. The above analysis makes it clear that if the Fed is correct in its assessment but is forced through political means to aim higher, then the inflation rate would accelerate (*b* would be less than zero).

On the other hand, if the Fed's critics are correct that potential growth is higher, then the Fed's error would show up, at least in the long run, in lower inflation. If inflation got too low then the Fed could adjust. Any negative effects on real GDP would be temporary—as in a temporary slowdown or a pause.

For the same reasons that there is no long-run trade-off between inflation and unemployment, a policy of underestimating potential GDP growth on the part of the monetary authorities would not have an effect on the long-run growth rate.

5   Conclusion

The intellectual foundations for the theoretical and empirical results about unemployment, inflation, and monetary policy that I have mentioned here have evolved from the rational expectations revolution of the 1970s. This is especially true if we acknowledge the contributions of Edmund Phelps and Milton Friedman as motivating the early work on rational expectations and wage and price behavior. Time inconsistency, the importance of credibility, the inflation-output trade-off in terms of fluctuations rather than levels and the view of monetary policy as a rule rather than pure discretion have all evolved from this research.

To the extent that these ideas influenced actual monetary policy, I think we already have seen some of the benefits. In the United States the disinflation policies of the early 1980s have been followed by a more credible policy aimed at keeping inflation low. One benefit of this monetary policy, of course, has been low inflation. But there is another important benefit: The U.S. economy has had a much-improved cyclical performance with two very long economic expansions separated by a relatively mild recession. Hence, it appears that this type of monetary policy is responsible not only for a long period of inflation stability, but also for a long period of remarkable output and employment stability.

3   Comments

BENJAMIN M. FRIEDMAN

Four pressing questions about the conduct of monetary policy have framed much of the discussion of this subject in recent years, and I would like to frame my remarks about Bob's and John's chapters in just those terms: First, does monetary policy affect real economic activity (as opposed to nominal magnitudes only)? Second, if monetary policy does affect real activity, should the central bank take those real effects into account in setting policy? Third, if so, how should the central bank go about doing this? And fourth, with or without attention to real effects, should the central bank set monetary policy according to a fixed rule? I will devote most of my comments to the first and last of these questions, with only brief comments on the two intermediate issues.

To begin, both Solow and Taylor agree that monetary policy does affect real economic activity, and I certainly share that view. But there is an important difference between their two chapters in this respect. Taylor makes clear that while he believes monetary policy has real effects in the short run, he is comfortable in assuming that these effects are not long-lasting. In other words, he accepts what we typically call the accelerationist (or natural rate) model. By contrast, although Solow makes clear that he is not comfortable with the accelerationist model, for the purpose of discussion about practical matters of monetary policy he goes ahead to assume it anyway. Solow's argument is that the evidence for the accelerationist model is extremely limited—in effect, to the experience of the United States since 1970. In particular, he argues that neither the U.S. experience before 1970 nor the experience of the European countries since then is in any way supportive of the accelerationist model.

This combination of contrast and agreement between Taylor's position and Solow's is, I believe, representative of consensus opinion among economists today. Some accept the accelerationist model as a valid description of macroeconomic behavior. Others doubt the model but accept it anyway as a working tool for policymaking purposes. I do not disagree with the consensus.

But it is worth pausing, nonetheless, to ask ourselves why we go ahead and make policy as if we accept this model even though the evidence for it is so slight. The answer that a typical economist would give, I suspect, is that in the absence of strong evidence to the contrary we are inclined to go along with the presumptions that the relevant theory provides. But what this answer really means is that we prefer to go along with the presumptions that the *simplest* theory provides. The distinction is important because we have plenty of theories, typically focusing on various kinds of either human or physical capital formation, according to which monetary policy plausibly has very long-lasting real effects. They are just not simple theories. (Whether these long-lasting effects are actually permanent is mostly beside the point for purposes of many aspects of monetary policymaking, but it is also not a matter on which we are likely to obtain persuasive evidence anyway. Our ability to distinguish econometrically between a permanent effect and one with a half-life of, say, sixty calendar quarters—not an unusual estimate in many kinds of empirical analysis—is suspect, to say the least.)

This preference for basing our policy analysis on very simple models is problematic in two senses: First, as an epistemological matter of how we learn and what we think in economics, it is troubling because we have many examples in which our simplest theories are patently inadequate to describe observed market phenomena. But it is especially problematic for purposes of monetary policy because our simplest theories also tell us that sustained inflation has no real costs. Hence the asymmetry: *Because of* simple theory, we choose to believe that monetary policy has no long-run effects on output. But we also believe, *in contradiction to* simple theory, that zero inflation is better than low inflation, and low inflation is better than moderate inflation. (Neither of these comparisons on the cost of inflation has much empirical support, although there is plenty of evidence to show that either low or moderate inflation is better than high inflation.)

As a question of policymaking, I too would proceed as if the accelerationist model were true, and go ahead to make policy on that basis. In this respect I disagree with neither Bob Solow nor John Taylor. But as a matter of economic science, I frankly find troubling not only that we have so little evidence on these important and crucially related questions but also that, when confronted with this absence of empirical evidence, we proceed to address them in diametrically opposite ways. The message for students of our subject, I think, is that the economics of monetary policy is hardly a closed field in which all important questions have been answered.

The second question that dominates the discussion of monetary policy today is whether the central bank should take effects on real activity into account in its policy decisions. Solow and Taylor both say yes, and I certainly agree. But it is important to point out that in many countries around the world today, as well as in the U.S. Congress, there is a tendency to believe the opposite. Specifically, a bill now pending before the U.S. Senate, under the sponsorship of the chairman of the Joint Economic Committee and co-sponsorship of the Senate majority leader, would designate price stability as the sole legitimate goal of U.S. monetary policy. Under this legislation, the Federal Reserve would have no authority to take the condition of real economic activity (employment, unemployment, real growth, and so on) into account in conducting monetary policy, except insofar as the state of the real economy would have a bearing on the likely behavior of prices. The Federal Reserve would also have no authority to take into account such matters as an impending financial crisis, either at home or abroad, or even the threatened collapse of the nation's banking system (again, except insofar as these events might have an impact on U.S. inflation). It is difficult to imagine that anyone would seriously want a country's central bank to behave in such a way, and both Solow's chapter and Taylor's provide cogent reasons for resisting such a proposal.

The third major question in today's discussion of monetary policy is how the central bank should take account of the real effects of its policy actions. Both Bob Solow (explicitly in his paper) and John Taylor (implicitly in the formula that he gives us for a monetary policy rule) answer that, apart from intentional efforts to raise or lower inflation from any given starting point, monetary policy should aim directly at whatever the central bank perceives to be the full-employment rate of real activity. Specifically, the central bank should not attempt to be "conservative" by aiming at a real activity rate that falls short of full employment.

Here again, it is important to point out that this is not a universally held view. Some economists—most prominently, Federal Reserve Chairman Alan Greenspan—have argued that the right approach is to stop short of the full-employment rate of output, lest monetary policy mistakenly push the economy into the inflationary range. The heart of this argument is a presumed asymmetry such that the risks associated with overshooting full employment are greater than those of undershooting—either because the costs of rising prices are greater than the costs of falling prices, or because inflation increases more easily than it slows down. It is important to point out that neither Solow's paper nor Taylor's rule supports this more "conservative" position, and the empirical literature does not support the kinds of asymmetry that it assumes.

Here, too, changes in the inflation performance itself have importantly altered the basis of the argument. A decade ago, and especially two decades ago, a plausible justification for such a "conservative" recommendation would have been the ongoing desire to slow inflation from its then-prevailing pace. As of 1995, however, the consumer price index is increasing at two-and-a-fraction percent per annum for the fourth year in a row. In the meanwhile, there is now broad agreement that the U.S. consumer price index overstates the true annual rate of price increase by a margin that is probably 1 percent and could easily be 1.5 percent. As a result, we have now reached the point at which the presumption that has dominated U.S. monetary policy-making for decades— that it is unnecessary to be specific about our inflation target, because *any* practical reduction in inflation is always desirable—is no longer an adequate basis for discussion.

Finally, the last of the four issues I want to address is whether monetary policy should follow a set rule. John Taylor, not only in his paper here but also in an impressive line of earlier research, argues that it should. Taylor argues for a monetary policy rule by appealing to the literature of time inconsistency and, in particular, by pointing to the benefits that this literature claims will ensue from precommitment of monetary policy and the resulting increase in policy credibility. Moreover, Taylor also acknowledges that in order to be practically useful, a rule has to be a simple rule. (James Tobin has made this point repeatedly.) Taylor's proposed formula for setting the federal funds rate, in response to observed fluctuations of inflation and real output, indeed qualifies as simple. But Taylor also acknowledges that no simple rule, including his, can cover all contingencies. He therefore is comfortable to contemplate that, from time to time, actual policy is going to deviate from the policy indicated by the rule.

I find all this very strange. The need for departures from any simple policy rule, in response to contingencies that such a rule was not designed to address, is precisely the ground on which many of us have long argued against having a monetary policy rule in the first place. Taylor's response is that the rule need not be confining; it is merely a rough guide, or baseline, that creates a presumption about what monetary policy should do in the absence of evidence or arguments to the contrary.

I am all in favor of having a rough guide to what monetary policy ought normally to do in the absence of reasons to the contrary, and as a semantic matter, if we now want to use the word "rule" to describe a rough, presumptive baseline of this sort, I suppose we are free to do so. But if the argument adduced for having a monetary policy rule is to take advantage of precommitment to achieve enhanced credibility, along the lines of the time inconsistency literature, then having a rough guide to what the central bank presumably will do unless there is a decent reason not to is simply not sufficient. One can argue for a fixed rule along the lines of the time inconsistency literature, *or* one can defend a flexible rule in the spirit of the contingencies argument. But the two are not the same, and it is wrong to appeal to both arguments simultaneously.

Moreover, to the extent that the argument on which Taylor leans to advocate a rule for monetary policy is the supposed advantage of precommitment under circumstances in which time inconsistency is a serious problem, the events of the last decade or so seem to me to have undermined this entire idea. Fifteen years ago, when high and rising inflation rates were the chief economic problem confronting most industrialized countries, the time inconsistency literature offered the interesting idea that this inflation was a natural consequence of discretionary monetary policymaking. But today that notion is far less persuasive. Most industrialized countries, including the United States, have succeeded in slowing their inflation, and in most cases they have done so under the same monetary policymaking institutions—importantly including discretion—to which the time inconsistency literature had pointed as the supposed source of the problem in the first place. Precommitment, by adopting a rule or otherwise, has typically not been part of the process. Hence it is somewhat ironic that Taylor is urging the Federal Reserve to adopt a monetary policy rule, principally on grounds stemming from the time inconsistency argument, just as the evidence of experience no longer warrants viewing time inconsistency as a major concern. (To the extent that similar time inconsistency arguments provide the main rationale for eschewing any attempt by monetary policy to take into account effects on the real economy, it is similarly ironic that the U.S. Senate should now be considering the proposal I described earlier.)

Finally, one further aspect of Taylor's advocacy of a monetary policy rule bears mention. As Taylor's figure 2.2 shows, in recent years there has been little recognizable difference between the rule that he recommends and what the Federal Reserve has been doing anyway. Is the object therefore merely to put a new label on what the Federal Reserve already does? Again, that is a semantic matter to which no one would seriously object. But most people think of the Federal Reserve's current and recent conduct of monetary policy as reflecting not a rule but discretion, and I believe they are right to think so. Similarly, most of the economists who have advocated monetary policy rules in the past—and certainly most of those who have been central contributors to the literature of time inconsistency, precommitment, and monetary policy credibility—would be startled to think that the main import of that entire line of research had been merely to provide new words to describe what our central bank, in its wisdom, has been doing all these years anyway.

JAMES K. GALBRAITH

Professor Taylor's paper has a central merit: He tells you where he stands. And while his rational expectations revolution will, I think, finally be remembered like 1917 rather than 1776, Taylor speaks, at least, with a revolutionary clarity of conviction.

As Orwell knew, language frames theory (especially during revolutions). To this end, Taylor conflates the "average level of unemployment," a neutral statistical notion, with the theoretically charged concept of the "natural rate of unemployment." Equally, he defines "potential GDP" as "the average level of real GDP." He asserts that the inflations of the 1970s "provide lessons about the impact of inflationary monetary policy." He does not feel any need to establish, for example with evidence, that the monetary policy was inflationary. How else, within the terms of his theory, could the inflations have happened? Words like "OPEC," "Vietnam," and "supply shock," though perfectly respectable when I learned them at Yale twenty years ago, have been purged from the language.

Some of Professor Taylor's arguments are asymmetric. He writes that the inflations of the 1970s prove that monetary policy can't cure unemployment. And these experiences "complement the lessons about the impact of a deflationary monetary policy from the devastating Great Depression of the 1930s when unemployment rose to more than 25 percent . . ." (p. 33). Have I read him right? Is he arguing that *deflationary* monetary policies *can cause* unemployment, but *expansionary* monetary policies *can't* cure it? (If both statements are correct, why doesn't the actual unemployment rate ratchet upward, without limit?) Revolutionary enthusiasm can get you into trouble, now and then.

Still, Taylor is clear on the key things. He seems to want an inflation target as the main objective of central bank policy today. To get to this point, he posits the complete exogeneity of potential GDP growth in his theoretical model, and therefore the long-run neutrality of money. This yields the natural rate hypothesis: no long-run trade-off between inflation and unemployment. Taylor presents evidence: a table showing five years when unemployment was about six percent and inflation varied a good deal, from as high as 9.0 to as low as 1.6 percent.

But Taylor does believe in a short-run trade-off. And since the natural rate identified in his way is higher than the actual rate of unemployment at present, inflation acceleration is a risk and monetary policy should be tight. Given the premise, the conclusions follow: short-run policies should stabilize unemployment at the natural rate. Taylor ends with a policy rule, according to which above-average GDP growth (at or below the natural rate of unemployment) and inflation above two percent should both be punished. This

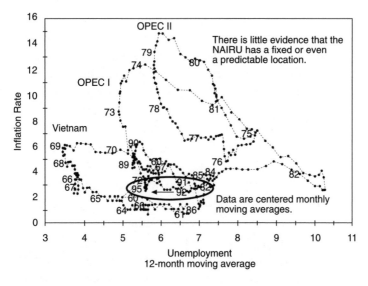

Figure 3.1
Inflation and unemployment

rule would have started the 1994 tightening in late 1992, and would maintain the present tight policy today, so long as the actual unemployment rate stays below 6 percent.

But is 6 percent really the natural rate of unemployment? Figure 3.1 makes the case against. Rather than the usual scatter of annual numbers, I plot centered twelve-month moving averages of inflation and unemployment for 1960 to 1994. The chart shows that eventually as unemployment fell inflation rose. But it never goes vertical at the same point. Conclusion: the "Accelerating Inflation Rate of Unemployment" (AIRU) shifts—it was perhaps 3.5 percent in 1969, 5 percent in 1974, perhaps 6 percent in 1979. But since 1982 the AIRU has been collapsing inward and very rapidly too; for the last four years (in the ellipse) we see no inflation acceleration for any reduction of unemployment. We cannot know where the AIRU is now, if it still exists (a deeper question to which we turn presently). But 6 percent seems most implausible on the evidence presently in hand.

Figure 3.2 shows, for each monthly unemployment rate since 1963, the *acceleration* of inflation over the year following. For the period through 1984, there is weak support for accelerationism, though the linear fit is mainly due to the disinflationary impact of high unemployment, which no one disputes, not the inflationary effects of prosperity. Since 1984, however, even that weak relationship between unemployment and inflation acceleration has disappeared.

In raising these doubts, I have plenty of respectable friends, including Professor Solow in the present exchange of papers. I think that Alvin Hansen, who favored full employment policy, would also have been among them. Hansen, after all, was a pragmatic Keynesian—as am I, when necessary and convenient. I should add, however, that my own theoretical views lie substantially to the left; I restrict myself to mainstream territory only because this is sufficient, under present circumstances, to win the point.[1]

Suppose Taylor's policy rule had been followed from 1992 forward. Possibly, had we done so, we could have gotten to 2 percent inflation (down half a point) and 6 percent unemployment (up half a point, or 600,000 lost jobs) that way.

But why? What would have been gained? As I have argued, Taylor's six percent NAIRU is probably wrong. And his two percent inflation target is simply arbitrary. Though I don't subscribe to the zero-inflation alternative, Taylor's

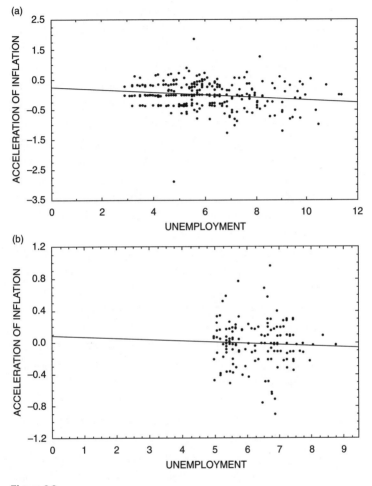

Figure 3.2
(*a*) Unemployment and inflation acceleration, 1960–1983 (high unemployment is the main cause of disinflation); (*b*) unemployment and inflation acceleration, 1984–1996 (the accelerationist impulse has disappeared)

argument for it even compares poorly to one offered to Congress in 1982 by John Rutledge (p. 32): "You may have wondered why God put zero in the middle of the numbers. That's because that's the optimal rate of inflation."

In fact, neither 2 percent nor 0 is any such thing. The welfare loss in moving from the present average 2.5 percent inflation rate to say 3 or 3.5 percent would be trivial. Conversely, a loss of jobs to reduce inflation below 2.5 percent seems senseless. To risk a recession to achieve such a goal would be irresponsible. Taylor's argument is of course that the moves are actually costless (in the long run). But here Milton Friedman's injunction that there is no free lunch might well be applied, for once.

I have less to say about Professor Solow's paper because I both agree with it and admire it. It is exactly the kind of argument I like to make, only better. It causes me some difficulty only because it threatens the position I thought I would safely hold on the left edge of this panel.

Professor Solow's approach is to take the policy positions offered by other people, in this case those who backed the 1994–1995 rise in interest rates, and to analyze them in terms of the models those people espouse. He shows that these models do not support relentless early intervention to fight inflation that may not exist or even threaten. He argues that given the uncertainties in the models, possible losses to employment and output should be considered. This is good logic and the plainest common sense.

My sources at the Federal Reserve tell me that some people there took a different view, or did as of early 1995 when this was first written. They said then that their favored inflation equation is more or less on track; we had passed the

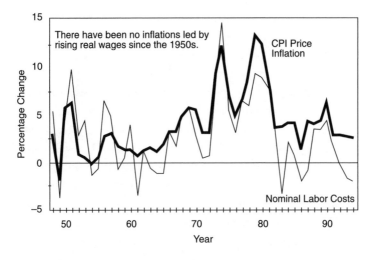

Figure 3.3
Inflation and labor costs, 1948–1994

NAIRU some time back and so, in Solow's phrase, "acceleration is just around the corner." Slow now, they said then, and we can have a soft landing.

Now, a year later, unemployment remains below 6 percent, and no inflation acceleration has occurred. Nairuvians are recalibrating their models, and the Federal Reserve should take heed. But there is also another problem, which gets at the logical structure underlying the concept of the NAIRU itself. It is illustrated in figure 3.3.

If we passed the NAIRU, real wages should be rising. Milton Friedman explicitly built the natural rate theory around real wage adjustment when he first presented it in 1968. But real wages have not risen, almost since that time, and they are not rising now. The old relationship between inflation and labor costs really has busted up since Reagan fired the air traffic controllers and he and Volcker overvalued the dollar. Prices may be rising at 2.5 percent, but money wages are fluctuating near 0 and real wages continue to fall.

How is this to be reconciled with unemployment below the natural rate? I don't believe it can be. Indeed, while today's gap between labor costs and prices is unprecedented, actually every period of rising inflation since 1960 has been led by prices, not wages (the sole exception being Richard Nixon's reelection drive in 1972). One might argue from this that unemployment has never fallen below the natural rate since the 1970s—and that these constructions were, in fact, irrelevant to the inflation that occurred.

On the other hand, getting inflation down again—the disinflationary reaction—has always required creating excess supply in product markets. This has been done in every case by creating a recession and forcing unemployment up. In history, that propensity to react by deflating, and not relentlessly accelerating inflation, is the "slippery slope." So it will be again. I'd feel a lot better about the soft landing metaphor if those who use it could point to historical examples.

I have in other work attempted to apply Professor Solow's methods to the Federal Reserve itself. I find that the Federal Reserve has nowhere officially spelled out its model. Indeed the original February 1994 interest rate hike was followed by testimony that there was no evidence of rising inflation currently or in the near future, no shocks and no errors of policy to be corrected. Instead, the Federal Reserve offered only the strange notion that the "real federal funds rate" was *per se* too low at zero. This justification quickly faded, and over the course of 1994, others were offered and then dropped. In early 1995 the Federal Reserve simply stopped raising rates, no explanation was given. Then–Vice Chairman Alan Blinder told *The New York Times* (March 18, 1985, page A37) that "if the central bank makes good decisions, we should not have any trouble explaining them." Apply the *modus tollens* to this conditional and you have my view exactly.

What should the Federal Reserve have done? My answer in 1994 was "nothing." Absent persuasive theory and evidence that a recession was worth risking, short-term interest rates should have been kept low. Long-term interest rates would then have adjusted downward, as the government promised repeatedly in 1993. Growth and investment might then have been a bit stronger in 1994 and 1995 than we actually experienced, and no economist can credibly claim that inflation would have been much higher. I don't think that an easier policy would have made any difference to inflation. And contrary to the inconclusive talk about the efficiency costs of higher inflation to which Taylor refers there would have been little economic harm if inflation had risen by a point or so.[2]

There would have been another advantage. The American middle class deserved some benefit from this economic expansion. Those who were previously unemployed are, of course, better off. And in 1993 the poor got some help, which the Congress since 1994 has done its best to take back. But the continuously employed middle class has received less than nothing so far: no increase of incomes, and yet a squeeze on their adjustable mortgages and a pinch on their savings invested as they largely are in stock and bond mutual funds. Low interest rates were a promise that the government could have kept. Raising them after the political developments of 1993, particularly the tax increases and program cuts in the deficit reduction package, was a breach of faith. The question of credibility is raised here in a way more profound, I think, than new classical economics allows for.

N. GREGORY MANKIW

This symposium was intended to be a debate about alternative views of monetary policy. But whenever symposium organizers invite two reasonable economists like Bob Solow and John Taylor, they always run the risk of agreement. And, indeed, when I read these two papers, I found myself agreeing with both of them much more than disagreeing. Therefore, what I would like to do is to take up a topic that Bob and John mention only briefly: the long-run effects of monetary policy.

Let me begin by reasserting a simple proposition: Monetary policy has important real effects in the short run, especially on output and unemployment, but these effects do not last in the long run. For both halves of this proposition, one can identify economists who argue with it. But I think it is fair to say that these economists are in the minority. Short-run non-neutrality and long-run neutrality are, I believe, as well accepted as any proposition in monetary economics.

The long-term issue I would like to address is the following: Given that money does not affect unemployment in the long run, what inflation rate should the Fed be aiming for?

To answer this question, let me recall that money is a unit of account. This is one of the three classic functions of money. To use a metaphor that goes back at least to Irving

Fisher, money is the yardstick with which we measure economic transactions. The job of the Fed, therefore, is a bit like the job of the Bureau of Standards: to make sure that this yardstick is a reliable tool of measurement.

To continue with Fisher's metaphor, imagine that we took a poll and asked people the following question: In 1995 the yard is 36 inches. How long do you think it should be in 1996 and 1997? If we asked this question of regular people, we would, first, have trouble getting them to take us seriously. Second, they would tell us that the yard should stay the same length—36 inches.

If we happened to poll an economist, however, we might get a very different answer. He would likely tell us that the length of a yard did not matter, as long as everyone knew what it was. He might go so far as to prove a neutrality theorem, showing that systematic changes in the length of the yard would merely alter all measurements proportionately without any real effects. By contrast, if the length of a yard were altered randomly, there would be short-run real effects, as people would take time to adjust to the unexpected changes in the unit of measurement.

Of course, the Bureau of Standards would not take the economist seriously. It is a great convenience to have a yard with constant length. And, for much the same reason, it would be a great convenience to have a dollar with constant real value. In other words, the Fed should aim for a long-run inflation rate of approximately zero.

In his paper, John Taylor endorses an inflation target of about two percent. He reasons that with upward biases due to measurement problems, two percent in the measured CPI may approximate price stability. I want to note, in this regard, that 2 percent is on the large side of the range of estimates of this upward bias. I have been told that Katherine Abraham of the Bureau of Labor Statistics thinks the upward bias is much smaller—less than 1 percent. This suggests that true price stability is pretty close to measured price stability.

In addition, it is not entirely clear to me whether price stability should be gauged in terms of the price of goods or the price of labor. Rather than aiming for zero inflation in the (bias-corrected) consumer price index, perhaps we should aim for zero inflation in the average hourly wage. The latter policy would, in the presence of technological progress, imply deflation as measured by the CPI. We are now close enough to price stability that the question "which price?" has become relevant.

If we accept the conclusion that zero inflation is the long-run ideal, we are naturally drawn to two other questions. First, is it worth the cost of getting there from here? And second, if zero is the long-run ideal, why has the average inflation rate over the past 30 years been much higher—about 5 percent per year?

Let me address the transition question first: Is it worth enduring a recession in order to get inflation from its current level (about 3 percent) down to zero?

The answer, I must admit, is: I don't know. Even though it is possible to point to several costs of inflation—shoe leather costs, menu costs, and so on—it is hard to know with much precision how large these costs are. In a recent paper, Martin Feldstein has tried to quantify some of the costs of inflation when inflation is at low levels. One large cost, he argues, arises from the interaction of inflation and taxes. Many economists, including myself, believe that current policy taxes capital income more heavily than is desirable. Moreover, because the tax laws are not indexed, that distortion rises with the inflation rate. In the second-best world in which we live, the Fed can indirectly reduce the distortion from capital-income taxation by reducing the rate of inflation. Feldstein offers some calculations to suggest that the tax-related cost of inflation is substantial.

Another cost of inflation is that it complicates personal financial planning. An important decision that all households face is how much of their income to consume today and how much to save for retirement. A dollar saved today and invested at a fixed nominal interest rate will yield a fixed dollar amount in the future. Yet the real value of that dollar amount—which will determine the retiree's living standard—depends on the future price level. Deciding how much to save would be much simpler if people could count on the price level in 30 years being similar to its level today. This cost of inflation has typically been ignored by economists, because self-selection and training makes most economists proficient at performing economic calculations. The general public, however, is not nearly as skilled. They understand, at an intuitive level, that inflation makes economic life needlessly complicated.

According to standard views of the inflation process (endorsed by Solow and Taylor), the cost of a disinflationary policy is temporary, whereas the benefits are permanent. Moreover, the benefits are most likely proportional to the size of the economy, so will grow over time. As Martin Feldstein argued over a decade ago, if our discount rate is low enough, we should be willing to endure a deep one-time recession to reduce inflation, even if the benefits per year of low inflation are not very large. As Fed Chairman, Paul Volcker appears to have bought this argument, and he is now considered a hero of central banking.

Bob Solow's chapter offers some unexpected support for this point of view. Early on in the chapter, he writes that "there is no good justification for inflicting higher inflation on the whole future in order to buy a temporary increment of consumption for one particular cohort of the ongoing population" (p. 7). Later in the chapter, he argues that there is nothing particularly asymmetric about the process determining inflation. These two conclusions together seem to imply that there is good justification for reducing inflation on the whole of the future at the cost of a temporary reduction of consumption for one particular cohort. This is not a view that Bob really holds, but it seems a logical implication of his arguments.

Let me now turn to my second question: If zero inflation is the right long-term target, why do we have ongoing inflation? There are several answers to this question.

One answer is given by the literature on time inconsistency. Once inflation expectations are formed and the private sector has acted on these expectations, it is tempting for the Fed to inflate in order to stimulate the economy. But, since people understand this temptation, they build it into their expectations. The result is higher inflation without lower unemployment.

The time-inconsistency literature offers a couple of solutions to this problem. One solution is the adoption of a policy rule, as John has discussed. Another solution is the appointment of conservative central bankers. This is the approach that the Carter administration chose with the appointment of Paul Volcker. It has continued since then under both Republican and Democratic administrations with the appointment and reappointment of Alan Greenspan.

Although I do think that time inconsistency is a true problem, let me suggest a second answer to the question of why we have ongoing inflation. Long-term inflation may be attributable to one of the most dangerous of human characteristics—wishful thinking.

It is natural to presume that what we would like to be true actually is true. Several years ago, they asked incoming Harvard Law students whether they expected to earn a place as an editor of the Harvard Law Review. An overwhelming majority thought they would, even though they all knew that less than 10 percent actually do make it. They were all overcome with wishful thinking.

In monetary policy, everyone would like to think that the unemployment rate can be pushed downward to some extent without causing inflation. We all wish for a low rate of unemployment consistent with price stability. To suggest that the natural rate of unemployment is high seems cold-hearted.

But wishing doesn't make it so. Wishful thinking is, I suspect, one reason that monetary policy has historically been excessively inflationary. It is always tempting to wish the natural rate of unemployment down. Of course, the result of this wishful thinking is, in the long run, higher inflation. To my mind, wishful thinking is as worrisome a problem for monetary policy as time inconsistency. I must admit that I detect a hint of wishful thinking in Bob Solow's suggestion that the Fed respond to uncertainty about the natural rate by stimulating more than it might otherwise.

One way to avoid wishful thinking is to adopt a policy rule, which (once adopted) precludes thinking of any sort. The policy rule that John Taylor proposes seems like a reasonable one, but I do wonder about its robustness to changes in the economy. In the past, Bob Hall and I have argued for a different kind of rule than the one John proposes. Hall and I have suggested that the Fed announce a target path for nominal GDP. The Fed would be deemed on target if the consensus forecast of private forecasters for nominal GDP a year or two hence were on the target path. Otherwise, it would adjust the money supply accordingly. Our simulations indicate that this rule would have historically resulted in real fluctuations about the same size as have been experienced over the post-war period, but with substantially more stable prices. In other words, a well-chosen policy rule would likely improve macroeconomic performance, but we should not expect miracles.

WILLIAM POOLE

There is much wisdom in the papers by John Taylor and Robert Solow. Nevertheless, this is a strange debate, because the authors talk past each other and do not sharpen points of disagreement. Professors Taylor and Solow agree about the single most important point—that in the long run the unemployment rate tends to return to the natural rate of unemployment. This rate depends on the structure of the labor market and government microeconomic policies but not on the rate of inflation.

I assume that my function is to sow seeds of conflict between the two debaters. There does seem to be some disagreement between them over the issue of "discretionary" monetary policy. This is the subject on which I'll concentrate first.

Second, there seems to be implicit conflict between the two authors on how to interpret uncertainty over estimates of the natural rate. Solow discusses this uncertainty at length, but Taylor pays minimal explicit attention to that topic. Taylor discusses at length the trade-off between inflation stability and output stability, but Solow does not mention that topic. These two points are more closely related than might at first appear, and both are closely related to the role of expectations in Phillips-curve analysis. I'll take up this topic after discussing policy rules.

Policy Rules, Policy Discretion

When it comes to the desirability of a policy rule, Taylor just has to be right. Solow would not want to fly in a plane whose pilot had been merely instructed to "use your best judgment, experiment, and feel your way along, fly wisely, incorporating all available information." When monetary policy pilots sit down at the controls, they should start from a base that tells them what the standard procedures are in various circumstances. To pass along accumulated experience from one generation to the next, we should be refining a policy rule, and that is exactly what Taylor is emphasizing in his remarks. To what extent a policy rule should be enacted into law is a different issue, which I will not address here.

Taylor and Solow both agree that monetary policymakers ought to be prepared to introduce special responses to special shocks, such as a stock market crash. These cases that seem to call for "discretion" in fact reflect the most clearly understood features of a monetary policy rule. The appropriate central bank response to a liquidity crisis was first clearly stated by Walter Bagehot in his 1873 book, *Lombard Street*. The details of the response differ from case to case—call these differences "discretion" if you like—but the basic principle of the central bank supplying additional liquidity to protect the normal functioning of the banking system and the money market is well established and well understood.

Consider some examples of successful Federal Reserve intervention to prevent liquidity disturbances from causing major financial problems: in 1970, the Penn-Central bankruptcy, which disrupted the commercial paper market; beginning in 1982, the international debt crisis that could have brought down several U.S. money center banks; in 1984, the bailout of Continental Illinois Bank to prevent disruption in the market for bank CDs and maintain confidence in money center banks in general; in 1987, policy easing in response to the stock market crash, to prevent all sorts of unknown horrors; in 1989, no response to the failure of Drexel Burnham Lambert because the markets were not threatened. These examples and others show that the clearest feature of our monetary policy is in fact central bank response to financial distress. Strangely, these are the cases that are most often discussed as "discretionary" in the rules-versus-discretion debate.

Unfortunately, what we lack is a well-tested policy rule for normal times. Taylor's enterprise is the right one, but I have my doubts about the rule he proposes. The two variables he concentrates on—output relative to trend and the inflation rate—are lagging indicators of the effects of monetary policy. What is remarkable about monetary policy after 1982 is that the Fed has acted much earlier than it would have in the past under similar circumstances. For example, the Fed started to push up interest rates in late 1986 before there was any indication that core inflation was rising and at a time when the unemployment rate was above 6.5 percent. The problem shows up in Taylor's figure 2.2. Fed policy was tighter than Taylor's rule in 1987, and fortunately so, given the lags in the effects of policy. Fed policy was slightly easier in 1990 and much easier in 1991–1992 than Taylor's rule. In retrospect, that ease was appropriate. I agree with Taylor that policy was too easy for too long in 1993, but his policy rule does not bend sharply up sooner than the actual Fed funds rate in early 1994.

A policy rule that feeds back from the observed levels of output relative to potential and the actual inflation rate is not going to be fully satisfactory because output, and especially inflation, lag the monetary stimulus that affects them. I do not have a better rule to offer, and I applaud Taylor's effort. Perhaps the best way to view Taylor's rule is that it provides a useful baseline from which monetary policy should depart when there is good and sufficient reason for doing so. The rule provides a good start from which to build a more refined rule.

Natural Rate Uncertainty, Inflation Expectations

Over recent months many economists have been surprised that inflation has not shown any significant rise over the past two or three quarters as the economy has overshot the consensus estimate of full employment. (Now, in December 1996, we can add six quarters of surprise and additional questions about the accuracy of earlier estimates of the natural rate of unemployment.) Solow's instinct is to emphasize that the natural rate of unemployment may be lower than we had thought. Taylor, as I read him, is more skeptical about making such a judgment on the basis of the information at hand.

In the spring of 1995 I thought that it was incorrect to conclude that the natural rate had declined, on the basis of a few quarters of data. In the absence of convincing evidence that the natural rate has fallen, Solow's concentration on the uncertainty over the natural rate could be an invitation to wishful thinking. Every point estimate is subject to uncertainty. Unless the loss function is asymmetric, the appropriate policy target is still the point estimate. I agree with Solow that we will learn as we go along—as we feel our way—but I think he is really sneaking an asymmetric loss function into his argument when he says that we should experiment with policy that pushes the unemployment rate below the best estimate of the natural rate. I don't see how to reconcile that position with his statement that "the goal of monetary policy ought to be to make approximately symmetrical errors" (p. 22). With that goal, in the Phillips-curve framework policymakers need to aim at the best available estimate of the natural rate if they want to keep the inflation rate unchanged. At least as important, policymakers must also act vigorously when necessary to contain inflation so that the market does not bid up inflation expectations.

Solow argues that we can afford to experiment with a policy that pushes the unemployment rate a bit lower because a rise in inflation, if it occurs, will be slow. The Fed will have time to reverse course and the inflation damage will be minimal, according to Solow. If inflation starts to rise, the genie can be stuffed back into the bottle at minimal cost.

I am not convinced. Solow's simulations are based on estimated models that do not treat expectations properly because expectations are captured imperfectly by distributed lags. My observation is that sharp increases in inflation have occurred in the past and, somehow, inflationary shocks always seem to arrive when the economy is at full employment or beyond. These inflationary shocks are endogenous in the sense that disturbances have inflationary consequences when the economy is vulnerable to inflation and not otherwise.

Business-cycle experience is clear that a significant increase in inflation—such as in 1956–1957, 1967–1968, 1973–1974, 1978–1979—is followed by a costly recession. The outside-shock explanation for these episodes is unsatisfactory because when we look at the details of these episodes it is clear that inflationary pressures were rising before the outside shocks. For example, inflation was clearly rising in the spring and summer of 1973 before the October war set off the oil-price shock. When driving too fast, a pothole might cause an accident that would not have occurred at a proper speed. Some might call the pothole the cause of the accident; I say that driving too fast is the cause because we have to allow for the possibility of potholes. It doesn't make sense to me to push the economy into the danger range in an effort to reduce unemployment by a few tenths of a percentage point, when the cost of being wrong is a recession that will increase the unemployment rate by two or more full percentage points.

In the spring of 1995, I was concerned about economic potholes. Writing in December 1996 I will concede that my forecast was wrong, and not for the first time. If the Fed had pursued a tighter policy, presumably inflation would have declined a bit instead of staying about the same.

Although Taylor and Solow agree on the key point that there is no long-run trade-off, they do not lock horns on the analysis of expectations. For about 25 years the accepted Phillips curve has been called the "expectations-augmented Phillips curve." The short-run Phillips curve takes the expected rate of inflation as given, and there is a trade-off between unemployment and inflation *given* the expected rate of inflation. In the long run, the expected rate of inflation adjusts, and there can be no persistent discrepancy between actual and expected inflation. That, plus the premise that behavior depends on real and not nominal magnitudes, is why the long-run Phillips curve is vertical.

Taylor emphasizes the importance of expectations in macroeconomic research over the past quarter century. Solow does not discuss expectations much at all. I believe that a viable hypothesis explaining the unemployment and inflation observations over the past three years is that the Federal Reserve has gained such credibility that the market does not expect a resurgence of inflation. In similar circumstances in the past both firms and workers expected that price and wage increases could be passed along, and so they were more ready to bid up prices and wages at an unemployment rate of 5.5 percent than they are today.

In explaining why inflation has not risen at an unemployment rate that has remained below 6 percent from late 1994 to this writing, some observers have emphasized that unions seem cowed or much less militant than in earlier years. That may be true, but it is also true that firms are more resistant to wage increases now than earlier. Despite clear signs of labor shortages in some geographic areas and some industries, firms are not bidding aggressively for labor. Firms realize that they are at risk if they let their costs get out of line and that it is hard to roll back wage increases once granted. These observations are consistent with powerful expectational effects.

The unemployment and inflation data since the 1960s—the data that lie behind the accepted estimate of a natural rate of 6 percent—do not include direct observation of expected inflation. Expected inflation is modeled through a distributed lag on actual inflation. As Taylor emphasizes, this is far from a foolproof method, because in an environment of price stability expectations of future inflation ought not to be related one for one with past inflation. Let me offer a further speculation: It is possible that the typical lagging behavior of the Federal Reserve from the mid-1960s until the early 1980s interacted with the aggregate unemployment rate to yield an upward biased estimate of the natural rate of unemployment. To see this point, suppose the natural rate has been 5.5 percent all along. (Solow emphasizes that the data do not reject such an estimate.) Now suppose the unemployment rate reaches 5.75 percent and the market expects the usual lag in the Fed's response, which permits the economy to overshoot 5.5 percent unemployment. In these circumstances, the inflation rate would start to rise because the expected inflation rate is rising, even though the unemployment rate is a bit above the natural rate. The upward shift of the Phillips curve because the expected rate of inflation is rising would not be picked up in a model in which expectations are not measured directly. Instead, the shift would be attributed to overshooting the natural rate, which would therefore be estimated by the model as higher than it really is.

I toss out this speculation not because I have evidence to support it but because it is important that we think carefully about expectations. Instead of concentrating on institutional changes that might explain a drifting natural rate, we should put at least equal effort into understanding whether changes in expectations, which have great theoretical importance in this model, could explain what we observe. I'll leave it to a Phillips curve expert to address this question: What would we have to believe about the behavior of inflation expectations in the past to be consistent with a constant natural rate of 5.5 percent since 1965 or thereabouts?

Now let me link this discussion to Taylor's analysis of the efficiency frontier for inflation stability and output stability. I think he pays entirely too little attention to the problem of getting to the frontier from the interior points that have characterized our history. Until recent years, Fed policy has yielded less stability for both inflation and output than the frontier indicates is possible. The main reason is that Fed policy has permitted inflation expectations to develop during the expansion phase of the business cycle, with the result that actual inflation rises more than would otherwise be the case, at the cost of subsequent recession to stuff the inflation genie back into the bottle. The enormous improvement in Fed policy over the past dozen years or so does not rest on fine tuning along the stability frontier but in getting much closer to that frontier. The real danger is that an effort to move us along the frontier, in the direction of more employment stability (or a lower average rate of unemployment à la Solow), will take us back toward the origin in Taylor's diagram, yielding less stability for both inflation and employment. Until market expectations of low and stable inflation become more solidly entrenched, points on Taylor's frontier toward more employment stability and less inflation stability may not be available to the Fed because an effort to get there instead unhinges inflation expectations and moves the economy inside the frontier.

In sum, I do not deny the validity of Solow's concerns over the accuracy of estimates of the natural rate but believe that he gives much too little attention to the importance of expectations in monetary policy. Maintaining low inflation, low inflation expectations, and Fed credibility is more important than feeling our way toward the correct estimate of the natural rate. If adverse expectations develop, then the Fed will have a problem no matter what the precise level of the natural rate might be.

I think the road to progress is not to emphasize uncertainty over estimates of the natural rate or the exogenous structural changes shifting the natural rate or fine-tuning along Taylor's stability frontier but interactions of private and Fed behavior and expectations. Market expectations of inflation, of future activity, and of Fed policy are all important. The fact that expectations are not mechanically linked to past realizations of inflation and unemployment means that we should be very careful about biases in econometric models of the Phillips curve.

Monetary policy debates, as evidenced by the Solow and Taylor papers and (I hope) my commentary, have become more nuanced and less ideological over the years. Most macroeconomists share a common core model, and most are well aware of the uncertainty over estimates of key parameters in the model. Some lean a bit one way, some another way. This fact makes a debate less exciting than in earlier days but is a sign of real progress in macroeconomics.

4   Responses

ROBERT M. SOLOW

I thank the discussants for their uniform kindness, and I wonder what it means. Jamie Galbraith fears that I have out-flanked him on the left, which was not my intention, and Greg Mankiw finds me reasonable, which, in a way, was my intention. Either (a) the distance between right and left ain't what it used to be, or (b) unlike Alvin Hansen, I am getting bland as I get older, or maybe both. Anyway, I do not have to defend myself except against suspicion of wishful thinking (which I categorically deny, though I am not above some thoughtful wishing, which is quite different). So I can take this occasion to comment in turn on some of the broader issues that arose in the discussion of both chapters.

Greg Mankiw, Jamie Galbraith, and Ben Friedman all call attention to a paradox that has bothered me and others for a long time. The attention that policymakers and others pay to mild inflation seems out of proportion to the identifiable costs imposed by mild inflation. I was careful in my chapter to say that the main reason for worrying about even fairly small inflationary incidents is that people dislike inflation. In a democracy, that is reason enough, even if there is a clear element of illusion in the dislike. But I cannot then see any good reason to risk recession in order to squeeze the last point or two of inflation out of the economy, if the current rate is already small enough that discontent has dwindled away.

Of course there are other things one can do: For instance, if it is the interaction of inflation and the tax system that causes distortion, indexing the tax system would be much safer than forcing the decreases in some nominal prices and wages that would be entailed by a zero-inflation policy. By the way, I see no merit in Mankiw's suggestion that nominal wages should be stabilized. Falling prices would impose the same calculational costs and larger transitional costs than rising prices, and for what?

The zero-inflation talk seems especially unmotivated in the light of Ben Friedman's correct observation that the same presumption of rational expectations that underlies the accelerationist model of inflation must also imply that much inflation would be anticipated and have no real effects beyond the more frequent use of logarithms.

I was a little surprised that Greg Mankiw could do no better than wishful thinking (not by me, not by him, but by others) to explain why observed rates of inflation average as high as five percent a year. I would nominate wars and adverse supply shocks as obvious suspects: wars, because governments are reluctant to tax adequately or to pay high interest rates and thus resort to monetizing the resulting deficits, and adverse supply shocks, because the attempt to neutralize them—in the inertia-ridden world we actually inhabit—runs the risk of depressing the level of output and employment substantially. (Having denied being a wishful thinker, I owe an answer to Mankiw's query about the justice of having the current generation bear the real costs of permanently reducing an excessively high rate of inflation. I think there is, in fact, an element of arbitrary injustice in that scenario. It speaks for gradualism and may also suggest that the Great Intergenerational Social Welfare Maximizer in the Sky, finding it hard to randomize over generations, would award the current generation the right to shift some costs to later generations by consuming more and investing less.)

William Poole's commentary is too extensive for me to make a careful point-by-point response. But I do want to confirm a couple of firm disagreements—at last!—and to indicate the direction a full reply would take.

First, we are certainly not in agreement about the natural rate of unemployment. I thought I had made it clear that I think the doctrine to be theoretically and empirically as soft as a grape. To say that in the long run the unemployment rate tends to return to the natural rate of unemployment is to say almost nothing. In the long run the unemployment rate goes where it goes. You can call where it goes the natural rate; but unless you have a more convincing story than I have seen about the length of the long run and the location of the natural rate, you are only giving a tendentious name to a vague concept. I said in my lecture that I was prepared to go ahead on the basis of natural-rate theory just so I could get on to the argument I wanted to make, and it could be made on that basis. The uncertainty about today's value of the natural rate is an important part of my skepticism. I feel obliged to remind Bill Poole that my skepticism does not make me an inflationist. As between a skeptic and a true believer, I think I know which one is more given to wishful thinking.

Second, we disagree about rules. Poole says that I would not want to fly in a plane whose pilot has been instructed merely to use good judgment, experiment, fly wisely, etc. Well, Poole would not want to bet on a basketball team whose coach had given the players a fixed set of rules at the beginning of the season: on the third possession of the second quarter, the off-guard should dribble twice, get to the baseline and shoot from the corner. With all due respect, that sort of analogy is not a serious argument. When I try to pass along experience from one generation to the next, I talk a lot about judgment, respect for evidence, etc. Poole talks about policy rules. That's OK, but, with all due respect, it is not a serious argument either. It may be that the reason we lack a well-tested rule for normal times is that there isn't one. More to the point, at any given moment central bankers and others may have clues that could not be incorporated into a rule. Of course they may be tempted to misuse discretion. One runs that risk in the belief that there are countervailing benefits.

Third, I meant what I said about the goal of monetary policy being to make symmetrical errors. I suspect Poole's talk about asymmetries is just the usual attempt to hint that anyone who disagrees is an inflationist. The asymmetry here is in nature or in history. Point estimates change with every new observation. It just happens that right now we are revising our point estimates of the safe unemployment rate downward. We have already experimented with unemployment rates higher than five and a half percent because that's the way the historical cookie crumbled. If inflation had started speeding up when the unemployment rate hit six and a half percent, the whole discussion would have taken a different form: A common belief would have been confirmed, not exploded.

Fourth, we come to expectations. I argued that the evidence suggests that mistaken policies, letting the unemployment rate get a little too high or a little too low, can be reversed at small cost. Dynamic responses do not appear to be asymmetric or large or unstable. I could be wrong, and Poole is right to be suspicious. But to rest the whole argument on expectations—that all-purpose unobservable—just stops rational discussion in its tracks. I agree that the expectations, beliefs, theories, and prejudices of market participants are all important determinants of what happens. The trouble is that there is no outcome or behavior pattern that cannot be explained by one or another drama starring expectations. Since none of us can measure expectations (whose?) we have a lot of freedom to write the scenario we happen to like today. Should I respond to Bill Poole by writing a different play, starring somewhat different expectations? No thanks, I'd rather look at data.

Finally, Ben Friedman's skepticism about the usefulness of a monetary rule seems entirely justified to me, for just the reasons he gives. I would only add the warning that a deep wish to evade the consequences of a rule when it becomes perverse would be likely to lead, in our culture, to economic policymaking by the courts as they find themselves forced to decide exactly what constitutes a violation of a legislated rule. I would prefer logarithms. As everyone seems to have observed, the Taylor Rule comes close to mimicking the discretionary behavior of the central bank we actually have. Does this speak well of the Rule, the Fed, or both?

To my mind, the most interesting part of John Taylor's paper is the proposal that there is a trade-off between the variance of the unemployment rate and the variance of the inflation rate. What does it mean? The variance of the unemployment rate is presumably a measure of the amplitude of the business cycle, and the variance of the inflation rate is just what it says it is. So we learn that a milder business cycle can be had only at the expense of greater irregularity of inflation, and whatever costs that entails.

The causal structure underlying this regularity is not clear; it might even be policy-induced, though not necessarily. Nor is it clear whether Taylor thinks of the average unemployment rate as some sort of equilibrium with mostly desirable properties. I am philistine enough not to accept that presumption without better proof than I have seen. Over any sample period, it is possible that the observed economy is usually below (or, for that matter, usually above) the socially optimal aggregate output and employment, in which case minimizing the variance of unemployment is not necessarily a very good guide to policy.

The regularity is interesting however it is to be interpreted. The near-cusp at the point where the two variances are equal is striking—almost too striking. If it is a robust finding, then it badly needs an explanation. No doubt a prior question is whether this finding is valid for other countries or for other periods in the United States, or indeed whether this sort of trade-off exists at all at other times and in other places. When it exists, does it have the same shape, and does it exhibit the same magic equal-variance point? Without knowing the answer to such questions one cannot know if Taylor's Rule is not just a way of instructing the Fed of the future to behave like the Fed of the past.

JOHN B. TAYLOR

I thank the discussants for their thoughtful reactions both to my opening presentation and to the presentation of Bob Solow. The discussants cover a wide range of current thinking on macroeconomics and monetary policy. In quite different ways, they illuminate areas of disagreement that exist among Bob Solow, me, and the discussants themselves.

By concentrating his remarks on monetary policy rules and on expectations, Bill Poole is probably successful in his aim of pointing out areas of "conflict between the two debaters." I think his airplane pilot analogy—emphasizing the purpose of policy rules in providing a standard set of procedures for monetary policy to follow—is a good one. I have found that new Federal Reserve Board members have been particularly interested in monetary policy rules because they find the rules useful in giving general guidance to their decisions, even though each probably would use discretion in responding to certain shocks not taken into account by a policy rule.

I also think Bill Poole is correct in his assessment that I place a greater emphasis than Bob Solow on the endogeneity of expectations to changes in policy. This is one reason why I am more concerned about a monetary policy that lets the "inflation genie" out of the bottle, a point to which I will return when commenting on Bob Solow's presentation. I was intrigued with Bill Poole's use of endogenous expectations theory to provide a new explanation of why inflation has been slow to pick up in the current cycle. According to Poole's explanation, people now expect the Fed to be more responsive to inflation, and this lowers inflation expectations, shifting the Phillips curve.

Given Bill Poole's support for policy rules *per se*, I welcome his questions about the particular policy rule I propose. It is my hope that such questioning will lead to refinements of such rules. I share his concerns that the policy rule might not be forward-looking enough. However, the rule does have some forward-looking features; for example, because output is positively correlated with future inflation, current output is an indicator of a future rise in the inflation rate. Even a policymaker concerned only with inflation would be wise to take output movements into account when setting interest rates.

Greg Mankiw suggests a much different alternative to the interest rate policy rule discussed in my presentation; he suggests a nominal GDP rule of the type he has recently written about with Bob Hall. In general, nominal GDP targeting calls for the central bank to keep the growth rate of nominal GDP in a given target range; the Hall-Mankiw proposal is to adjust the instruments of monetary policy (the money supply or the interest rate) depending on whether the forecast of nominal GDP growth is above or below target.

However, a nominal GDP target does not specify *how* the instruments of policy should be changed in order to achieve that target. Similarly, a target for the inflation rate or the price level leaves open what the central bankers should do with the instruments. To use Bill Poole's airplane example again, setting targets without specifying policy rules for the instruments is like telling an airplane pilot to keep the plane at 20,000 feet, with a due west heading, without specifying how to adjust the speed, elevation, or direction of the plane. Monetary policy, like flying a plane, requires technical expertise in the use of instruments. Macroeconomics has much to say about how the instruments affect the course of the economy, and policy rules stated in terms of the instruments can be useful in, at least, giving good standard procedures for central bankers to follow.

Ben Friedman also devotes much of his comments to the issue of policy rules. He seems to suggest that the sole justification for policy rules is the time-inconsistency problem, and he then goes on to question that justification. However, the time-inconsistency problem is only one of many reasons for using policy rules. As stated in my presentation, economists need to stipulate future policy actions—through a policy rule—in order to evaluate the effects of policy. Moreover, policy rules reduce uncertainty and are a good way to give advice to policymakers (this is Bill Poole's point about the need to "pass along experience from one generation to another"). Finally, policy rules can also provide better accountability.

I disagree with Ben Friedman's view that it is strange for policy to both use a policy rule and exercise some discretion in how the rule is employed. Consider three policy regimes. In regime 1, a policy rule is used for all decisions, so that the policy rule "explains" 100 percent of interest-rate variance. In regime 2, the policy rule is used as a general guideline with discretionary deviations occurring in special cases in such a way that about 85 percent of the interest rate variance is explained by the policy rule. In regime 3, there is pure discretion; the policy rule is ignored. In other words, regime 1 is pure rule, regime 2 is a mixture of rules and discretion, and regime 3 is pure discretion.

In my view, the second regime is both feasible and realistic with current knowledge and dominates the third regime. It is superior to the third regime because it gives greater certainty and predictability about policy and has many of the other advantages of a policy rule mentioned above. It remains to be seen whether policy rules can ever be used as in the first regime, but at this time the mixture seems less strange to me than either the pure rule regime 1 or the pure discretionary regime 3.

In describing her recent experience on the Federal Reserve Board, Janet Yellen indicates how natural and useful it is to have a policy rule to give general direction while at the same time being on the lookout for the need to deviate from the rule in special circumstances. This sounds a lot like regime 2. I agree with Yellen that, at least with our current knowledge, events like the 1987 stock market crash require the Fed to depart from the rule, so that some discretion is still necessary in working with a rule.

Future research can be very useful in order to refine policy rules and to enable policymakers to better use them. I think that Milton Friedman's remarks about his k-percent rule are particularly appropriate:

I should like to emphasize that I do not regard my particular proposal as a be-all and end-all of monetary management, as a rule which is somehow to be written in tablets of stone and enshrined for all future time. . . . I would hope that as we operated with it, as we learned more about monetary matters, we might be able to devise still better rules, which would achieve still better results.[1]

Jamie Galbraith is highly critical of the general approach I use in analyzing monetary policy, including the natural rate hypothesis which is a key element of the approach. In my presentation I responded to recent work by Fair and Eisner who have similar criticisms of the natural rate hypothesis; in my view there is overwhelming evidence that higher inflation does not bring lasting lower unemployment.

I believe that some of Jamie Galbraith's criticism may be due to semantic issues. For example, the term potential GDP as currently used in most textbooks and by practical macroeconomists means the average level of GDP, about which actual GDP fluctuates. The growth of potential GDP is due to the growth of supply over time. According to this definition, it is possible for real GDP to be above potential. Although the terminology may not be true to the dictionary definition of "potential," this is not the first inconsistency between an economic term and everyday usage. However, I believe that Jamie Galbraith's view that monetary policy can raise the growth rate of potential GDP by being more stimulative is contradicted by the same evidence that proves the natural rate property.

There may also be some semantic confusion concerning the lessons from the Great Depression; the modern macroeconomic view that I described in my presentation does not imply that policy in the 1930s was good, as Jamie Galbraith suggests it does. On the contrary, in the 1930s unemployment was clearly way above the natural rate, and any reasonable monetary policy should have allowed for greater aggregate demand. Moreover, I do not see any inconsistency in emphasizing the hard policy lessons of both the Great Depression of the 1930s and the Great Inflation of the 1970s. These lessons are complementary warnings of the great harm that policy errors—in two different directions—can cause.

Bob Solow's paper raises one of the most important issues facing monetary policymakers: how and when to start taking action to raise interest rates in order to rein in inflation when it is rising or is expected to rise. Constant money growth policy rules have an answer to this question: When inflation (and the price level) rises, real money balances fall and interest rates automatically rise. The monetary policy rule I discussed in my opening presentation also gives an answer: Raise interest rates when inflation or output begin to rise.

Solow uses economic reasoning, econometric estimates, and computer simulations to support his view that there are reasons to delay monetary tightening beyond what is suggested by the genie metaphor—that we should be worried about reversing an inflation that has already begun. Because Solow is performing his policy analysis in a largely "discretionary mode" without reference to any policy rule, it is not clear whether his suggested wait-and-see delay would bring about a policy response sooner or later than either of the two policies mentioned in the previous paragraph. However, I worry that within the discretionary regime implied by his analysis, the delay would be too long.

The history of the business cycle at least since World War II is that every recession has followed a period in which inflation had already begun to rise. In other words, reversing this rise in inflation has, at least during this historical period, been very difficult and painful. Unfortunately, after a rise in inflation, soft landings have been the anomaly and recessions the norm.

However, since the high and volatile inflation of the '70s ended, recessions have been far less frequent and severe than earlier. Since 1982 the United States has experienced two record-breaking economic expansions separated by a relatively mild national recession. Keeping the inflation genie in the bottle has been a pretty good recession deterrent.

This experience leads me to the view that a monetary policy which risks a rise in inflation also risks another recession, a risk that would be of great concern to me even if the higher inflation were not itself costly (which it is). Moreover, because the computer simulations reported by Solow do not apparently incorporate the impact of a Fed delay and higher inflation on expectations of future inflation and thereby on the dynamics of inflation, they do not alleviate my concerns very much. I would err on the side of not letting the inflation get started.

5   Rejoinder

JOHN B. TAYLOR

In his response to my presentation, Bob Solow concentrates on the trade-off between the variability of inflation and the variability of unemployment. He indicates that the causal structure of the trade-off is not clear from my verbal presentation.

A more technical explanation of this trade-off, along with a description of how it was derived from an estimated econometric model, is found in Taylor (1979). The "causal structure" which underlies the trade-off is the macroeconomic model described in that paper, a model with rational expectations in which prices and wages respond slowly to changes in demand. But this type of trade-off is also implied by virtually any model in which an "expectations-augmented" Phillips curve appears, as I tried to show in a graphical analysis in Taylor (1994) and in the verbal description in my presentation at the Hansen symposium.

The trade-off does not assume that the natural rate of unemployment is optimal. However, because no long-run Phillips curve trade-off is assumed, monetary policy cannot be used to lower the actual unemployment rate below the natural unemployment rate permanently.

Macroeconomic policy has to be efficient before we are actually on the frontier of this trade-off. In my view, the history of macroeconomic policy indicates that we have usually been inside the trade-off, at least until recently, making estimation difficult. In other words, a policy that does not keep aggregate demand as stable as possible could be improved in a way that would increase both employment and inflation stability—moving us closer to the frontier of the trade-off.

I too am worried about the policy invariance of such a trade-off, though the purpose of my using a fully specified economy-wide model when estimating the trade-off in Taylor (1979) was to reduce the possibility of its being policy-induced.

I pointed out at the start of my presentation that estimates of the trade-off have been provided by other researchers but should still be viewed as preliminary. I agree that the shape is interesting, which is why I brought attention to it in my presentation. But, I also agree that the empirical estimates ought to be studied much more thoroughly with data from different countries and different periods.

Finally, and this is very important, the optimality and usefulness of a monetary policy rule of the type I discussed in my presentation do not depend on whether this particular numerical estimate of the trade-off is accurate, though Bob Solow implies the contrary in his closing sentence. True, that such a short run trade-off exists is important for policy, but the exact location of the frontier is fortunately less important. In fact, the properties of a policy rule like this should be robust to a much wider range of models than would be implied by a single point estimate of the trade-off.

ROBERT M. SOLOW

In reply to John Taylor, I would say only two non-provocative things. First, I should have thought of going back to his justly well known 1979 paper to find the deeper roots of his variability trade-off. I promise to do that. One can see how it might arise as a sort of partial-reduced-form from a larger model. The details will be interesting as an indicator of robustness. Second, I can see how the last sentence of my comment might be misleading. There is no need to connect the variability trade-off with the utility of the Taylor Rule. All I meant to say—but didn't, quite—is that an economy with different underlying behavior—manifested, perhaps, in the trade-off—might want a different rule (if it wanted a rule at all).

Contributors

Benjamin M. Friedman
William Joseph Maier
Professor of Economics
Harvard University

James K. Galbraith
Professor, Lyndon B.
Johnson School of Public
Affairs and Department of
Economics
University of Texas at
Austin

N. Gregory Mankiw
Professor of Economics
Harvard University

William Poole
Professor of Economics
Brown University

Robert M. Solow
Institute Professor of
Economics Emeritus
Massachusetts Institute of
Technology

John B. Taylor
Mary and Robert Raymond
Professor of Economics
Stanford University

Notes

Chapter 2

This research was supported by a grant from the National Science Foundation at the National Bureau of Economic Research and by the Center for Economic Policy Research at Stanford University. This chapter was revised again in May 1996.

1. Potential GDP is defined here as the average level of real GDP; it is assumed to grow smoothly over time according to an aggregate production function, as labor, capital, and technology increase. Real GDP fluctuates around potential GDP.

2. For a graphical derivation of this trade-off see Taylor 1994. In previous work (including Taylor 1994) I have plotted out *in*stability on the horizontal axis and inflation *in*stability on the vertical axis, so that the trade-off curve is reversed from that in figure 2.1. For ease of comparison with production possibilities curves I chose to plot "goods" rather than "bads" on the axes in figure 2.1.

3. Difficulties in measuring money and finding a stable money demand function are the reasons interest rates are favored over the money supply in these simulations, as expected from William Poole's famous (1970) paper. In my view if there were a way to automatically adjust the measures of money so that they were a more reliable indicator of monetary policy, then the money supply would be a superior instrument. Benjamin Friedman (1988) examines the risks of an interest rate oriented monetary policy in comparison with a money supply policy. See Feldstein and Stock 1994 for a new approach to making a money supply policy work in practice.

Chapter 3

1. In my preferred theory, potential real GPD is endogenous and not readily located *ex ante*, money is not neutral, and there is no natural rate of unemployment that can serve as a useful guide to policy. Overly restrictive policies can damage the accumulation of physical and human capital and have a complex effect on the accretion of new technology, as old technologies are destroyed in the slump and new ones introduced in the upswing. A vigorous cycle isn't ideal, but it's better to have uncontrolled investment booms sometimes than never to grow vigorously at all. Steady high growth as in Japan for forty years or so until recently is better still, but that requires active policy management, as the Japanese are discovering now.

2. And what should the Federal Reserve do now? Lower rates and keep them down. Let the economy grow until there are credible signs of reaching limits, and then evaluate the situation.

Chapter 4

1. See Milton Friedman (1962, pp. 54–55).

References

Ball, Laurence M. 1994. "What Determines the Sacrifice Ratio?" In N. Gregory Mankiw (ed.), *Monetary Policy*. Chicago: University of Chicago Press for the National Bureau of Economic Research.

Ball, Laurence M. 1997. "Disinflation and the NAIRU." In Christina D. Romer and David H. Romer (eds.), *Reducing Inflation: Motivation and Strategy*. Chicago: University of Chicago Press.

Barro, Robert, and David Gordon. 1983. "Rules, Discretion, and Reputation in a Model of Monetary Policy." *Journal of Monetary Economics* 12: 101–122.

Brainard, William C. 1967. "Uncertainty and the Effectiveness of Policy." *American Economic Review* 57: 411–425.

Bryant, Ralph, Peter Hooper, and Catherine Mann. 1993. *Evaluating Policy Regimes: New Empirical Research in Empirical Macroeconomics*. Washington, D.C.: Brookings Institution.

Debelle, Guy, and Stanley Fischer. 1994. "How Independent Should a Central Bank Be?" In Jeffrey C. Fuhrer (ed.), *Goals, Guidelines, and Constraints Facing Monetary Policymakers*. Boston: Federal Reserve Bank of Boston.

Eisner, Robert. 1997. "A New View of the NAIRU." In Paul Davidson and Jan Kregel (eds.), *Improving the Global Economy: Keynesianism and Growth in Output and Employment*. Cheltenham: Edward Elgar.

Fair, Ray. 1996. "Testing the Standard View of the Long-Run Unemployment-Inflation Relationship." Cowles Foundation discussion paper, no. 1121.

Feldstein, Martin. 1979. "The Welfare Cost of Permanent Inflation and Optimal Short-run Economic Policy." *Journal of Political Economy* 87: 749–768.

Feldstein, Martin. 1997. "The Costs and Benefits of Going from Low Inflation to Price Stability." In Christina D. Romer and David H. Romer (eds.), *Reducing Inflation: Motivation and Strategy.* Chicago: University of Chicago Press.

Feldstein, Martin, and James H. Stock. 1994. "Measuring Monetary Growth When Financial Markets Are Changing." National Bureau of Economic Research, working paper no. 4888.

Fischer, Stanley. 1993. "The Role of Macroeconomic Factors in Growth." *Journal of Monetary Economics* 32: 485–512.

Friedman, Benjamin. 1988. "Monetary Policy without Quantity Variables." *American Economic Review* 78: 440–445.

Friedman, Milton. 1962. *Capitalism and Freedom.* Chicago: University of Chicago Press.

Friedman, Milton. 1968. "The Role of Monetary Policy." *American Economic Review* (March): 1–17.

Fuhrer, Jeffrey. 1995. "The Persistence of Inflation and the Cost of Disinflation." *New England Economic Review* (January / February): 3–16.

Fuhrer, Jeffrey, and Brian Madigan. 1994. "Monetary Policy When Interest Rates Are Bounded by Zero." Presented at the Center for Economic Policy Research—Federal Reserve Bank of San Francisco Conference, March 1994.

Galbraith, John Kenneth. 1965. "How Keynes Came to America." In *Economics Peace and Laughter.* Reprint, Boston: Houghton Mifflin, 1971.

Gordon, Robert J. 1994. "Where is the NAIRU?" Presented at a meeting at the Board of Governors of the Federal Reserve System.

Gordon, Robert J. 1997. "The Time-Varying NAIRU and Its Implications for Economic Policy." *Journal of Economic Perspectives* 11: 11–32.

Hall, Robert E., and N. Gregory Mankiw. 1994. "The Use of a Monetary Aggregate to Target Nominal GDP." In N. Gregory Mankiw (ed.), *Monetary Policy.* Chicago: University of Chicago Press.

Hansen, Alvin Harvey. 1960. *Economic Issues of the 1960s.* New York: McGraw-Hill.

Kydland, Finn, and Edward Prescott. 1977. "Rules Rather Than Discretion: The Inconsistency of Optimal Plans." *Journal of Political Economy* 85: 473–492.

Lindbeck, Assar. 1993. *Unemployment and Macroeconomics.* Cambridge, Mass.: The MIT Press.

Lucas, Robert E., Jr., and Thomas J. Sargent. 1981. *Rational Expectations and Econometric Practice.* Minneapolis: The University of Minnesota Press.

Medoff, James, and Andrew Harless. 1994. "Undetected Slack." Presented at a meeting at the Board of Governors of the Federal Reserve System.

Meyer, Laurence H. 1996. "Monetary Policy Objectives and Strategy." Board of Governors of the Federal Reserve Board, National Association of Business Economists, Boston, Mass., September 8, 1996.

Motley, Brian. 1994. "Growth and Inflation: A Cross-Country Study." Prepared for the Center for Economic Policy Research—Federal Reserve Bank of San Francisco Conference, March 1994.

Owyong, Tuck Meng. 1996. "Price Variability, Output Variability, and Central Bank Independence," Center for Economic Policy Research, Stanford University discussion paper.

Phelps, Edmund S. 1967. "Money Wage Dynamics and Labor Market Equilibrium." *Journal of Political Economy* 75: 678–711.

Phelps, Edmund S. 1994. *Structural Slumps.* Cambridge, Mass.: Harvard University Press.

Phillips, A. W. 1958. "The Relationship between the Unemployment Rate and the Rate of Change in Money Wage Rates in the United Kingdom, 1861–1957." *Economica* 25: 283–299.

Poole, William. 1970. "Optimal Choice of Monetary Policy Instruments in a Simple Stochastic Macro Model." *Quarterly Journal of Economics* 84: 197–216.

Rutledge, John. 1981. "Outlook for Recession." Testimony presented to Joint Economic Committee hearing, October 21, 1981.

Sargent, Thomas J. 1971. "A Note on the 'Accelerationist' Controversy." *Journal of Money Credit and Banking* 3: 721–725.

Staiger, Douglas, James H. Stock, and Mark W. Watson. 1997. "How Precise Are Estimates of the Natural Rate of Unemployment?" In Christina D. Romer and David H. Romer (eds.), *Reducing Inflation: Motivation and Strategy.* Chicago: University of Chicago Press.

Taylor, John B. 1979. "Estimation and Control of a Macroeconomics Model with Rational Expectations." *Econometrica* 47: 1267–1286.

Taylor, John B. 1992. "The Great Inflation, the Great Disinflation, and Policies for Future Price Stability." In Adrian Blundell-Wignall (ed.), *Inflation, Disinflation, and Monetary Policy*. Sydney: Reserve Bank of Australia and Ambassador Press.

Taylor, John B. 1993. "Discretion versus Policy-Rules in Practice." *Carnegie Rochester Conference Series on Public Policy* 39: 195–214.

Taylor, John B. 1994. "The Inflation/Output Variability Trade-off Revisited." In Jeffrey Fuhrer (ed.), *Goals, Guidelines, and Constraints Facing Monetary Policymakers*. Boston: Federal Reserve Bank of Boston.

Tobin, James. "Alvin Hansen and Public Policy." *The Quarterly Journal of Economics* 90 (February 1976): 32–37.

Yellen, Janet. 1996. "Monetary Policy: Goals and Strategy." Board of Governors of the Federal Reserve System, National Association of Business Economists, Washington, D.C., November 13, 1996.

Index

Abraham, Katherine, 74
Accelerating Inflation Rate of
    Unemployment (AIRU) shifts,
    65–66, 69
Accelerationist model
  alternative to, 8–13
  evidence for, 5, 56, 66
  inflation and, 5–7, 18–19, 90
  monetary policy and, 56–57
  natural rate of unemployment in,
    5
  neutral rate of unemployment in,
    5–9, 13
  supply-demand balance and, 5
  unemployment and, 8–13
  United States economy and, 5–6,
    56
Aggregate demand shocks, 40
AIRU shifts, 65–66, 69
"Alpha equals one" hypothesis,
    34–35
Average level of unemployment,
    63

Bagehot, Walter, 80
Ball, Laurence, 11–13, 41
Barro, Robert, 44–45
Beveridge Curve, 27
Blinder, Alan, 20, 71

Brainard, William, 28
Bryant, Ralph, 46
Bureau of Standards, 73–74
Business cycle fluctuations, 39–40,
    83, 100–101

Canada, 8, 33
Carter administration, 76–77
Central banks
  GDP and, 53
  interest rates and, 50–52
  liquidity crisis and, 80
  monetary policy and, 55, 58–63
  neutral rate of unemployment
    and, 11–12
  oil shock and, 10–11
  Owyong's work and, 42–43
  policymaking of, 16–17, 58
  real economy and, 55, 59
  set rule of monetary policy and,
    55, 60–63
  unemployment and, 17, 20
Competition, international, 27–
    28
Congressional Budget Office, 18
Constant money growth policy
    rules, 100
Consumer Price Index (CPI), 1, 24,
    60, 74

Continental Illinois Bank bailout, 80
Costs, 2, 69–70. *See also* Price
  levels
CPI, 1, 24, 60, 74
Creeping inflation, 1

Debate of monetary policy
 comments on, 55–88
  Friedman, 55–63
  Galbraith, 63–72
  Mankiw, 72–78
  Poole, 1, 78–88
  Solow's response to, 89–95
  Taylor's response to, 95–101
  rejoinders to, 103–105
  Solow's view, 1–28, 105
  Taylor's view, 29–54, 103–105
  trend in, 88
Debelle, Guy, 42
Deceleration, 22
Deficit reduction package, U.S., 72
Deflation, 33–34, 46
Depression. *See* Great Depression
  (1930s)
Deregulation, 10
Disinflation, 11–12, 21, 70, 75–76
Downward stickiness, 2
Drexel Burnham Lambert failure,
  80

Econometric models, 88, 103
Economy. *See also* Great Depres-
  sion (1930s)
  real, 3–4, 6, 55–56, 59
  recession in, 1–2, 74, 83–84, 90
  United States, 5–6, 54, 56
EFTA countries, 8–9
Eisner, Robert, 15–19, 24
Employment Cost Index, 26–27
Employment, full-time rate of, 59,
  66
Europe, 8–10, 35–36
European Community, 8–9

European Free Trade Area (EFTA)
  countries, 8–9
Expectations-augmented Phillips
  curve, 84, 103

Fair, Ray, 34
Federal funds, 47–49, 70
Federal Reserve
  credibility of, 84, 87
  federal funds and, 48–49
  inflation and, 53, 68–69, 72–73,
    85–86
  interest rates and, 16, 70–71
  job of, 73
  lagging behavior of, 85–86
  liquidity crisis and, 80
  monetary policy and, 58, 62–63
  nominal GDP and, 78
  policymaking of, 16, 58, 70–71, 98
  set rule of monetary policy and,
    62–63
  stability for inflation and output,
    86–87
  stock market break (1987) and, 48
  successful intervention by, 80
  unemployment and, 17, 85–86
Feldstein, Martin, 74–76
Fiscal policy, 3–4
Fischer, Stanley, 36, 42
Fisher, Irving, 72–73
France, 8, 10
Friedman, Benjamin M., 55–63,
  89–90, 93, 97–98
Friedman, Milton, 31, 53–54, 68–
  69, 98–99
F-statistics, 23
Fuhrer, Jeffrey, 21, 33
Full employment policy, 59, 66

Galbraith, James K., 63–72, 89, 99–
  100
GDP
  actual, 99

average level of, 99
central banks and, 53
federal funds and, 47–48
fluctuations in, 43–44, 99
inflation and, 37, 47–48
interest rates and, 52
money supply and, 49–50
nominal, 78, 96
potential, 30, 36, 44, 47, 50–53, 63–64, 99
real, 30, 37–39, 40–41, 43–44, 46–51, 63, 99
shocks and, 40–41
Genie-and-the-bottle response to inflation, 16–17, 23, 100–101
Germany, 8–10
Gordon, David, 45
Gordon, Robert, 7–8, 13–14, 16–19, 24, 26
Great Depression (1930s), 29, 33, 39, 64, 99–100
Great Inflation (1970s), 39, 100
Greenspan, Alan, 59, 77
Gross domestic product. *See* GDP

Hall, Bob, 78, 96
Hall-Mankiw proposal, 96
Hansen, Alvin, 1–3, 66, 89
Harless, Andrew, 27
Help-wanted index, 27
Hooper, Peter, 47

Impulse-reaction function, 23–24
Income per capital, 36
Inflation. *See also* Accelerationist model; Unemployment-inflation trade-off
acceleration of, 16–18, 26–27, 66, 83
in Canada, 33
concern over, 89–90
costs of, 74–75
creeping, 1
expectations, 81–88

Federal Reserve and, 53, 68–69, 72–73, 85–86
fluctuations in, 40, 42
GDP and, 37, 47–48
genie-and-the-bottle response to, 16–17, 23, 100–101
Gordon and, 17–18
Hansen's approach to, 1–3
impulse-response function and, 23–24
income per capita and, 36
interest rates and, 52
in Japan, 46
labor costs and, 69–70
lagged, 23, 35
long-lag response to, 16–18
long-term, 77
low levels of, 33–34
measuring, 46
model, 24–26
monetary policy and, 54, 62, 80–81
negative, 34
neutral rate of unemployment and, 7
of 1970s, 39, 100
persistency of, 21
Phillips Curve and, 86
pragmatism in discussion of, 4
price index in measuring, 14
productivity growth and, 36–37
pushing on a string response to, 23
rational expectations model of, 33–34
real economy and, 3
recession and, 83–84, 90
sacrifice ratio and, 21
sources of, 2, 5–6
stability, 38–41, 43–44, 47, 86–87
target, 34, 45–46, 60, 64, 73–74, 76, 96–97
tax system and, 90
time series of rates, 21–22
unemployment and, 6–7, 37, 65, 85

Inflation (cont.)
  in United States, 32–33
  zero, 31, 34, 66, 68, 74, 76, 90
Interest rates
  central banks and, 50–52
  equilibrium, 52
  Federal Reserve and, 16, 70–71
  GDP and, 52
  inflation and, 52
  long-term, 71
  in money equation, 49–52
  nominal, 33, 50–51
  real, 33, 51–52
  rise in (1994–1995), 68
  rule, 45–53
  short-term, 16, 49, 71

Japan, 46
Job-vacancy rate, 27

Keynesian revolution, 29
k-percent money growth rule, 51, 98–99
Kydland, Finn, 44

Labor costs, 69–70
Labor market, 6, 9–10, 36
Lindbeck, Assar, 35
Liquidity crisis, 80
Long-lag response to inflation, 16–18
Lucas critique of policy evaluation, 45

Macroeconomics, 3–4, 11, 39–40, 44, 84, 97
Madigan, Brian, 33
Mankiw, N. Gregory, 72–78, 89–91, 95
Mann, Catherine, 47
Medoff, James, 27

Middle class, American, 71
Monetary policy. See also Debate of monetary policy
  accelerationist model and, 56–57
  aggregate demand shocks and, 40–41
  asymmetry in, 22
  central banks and, 55, 58–63
  constant money growth policy rules, 100
  credibility about, 45
  criticism of, 53
  deflationary, 33, 64
  discretionary, 3, 79–81
  dual benefits of, 30
  effects of, 45
  evaluation of, 44–45
  expansionary, 3, 64
  Federal Reserve and, 58, 62–63
  goals of, 22, 30, 58, 92
  inflation and, 54, 62, 80–81
  lags, 20–23
  macroeconomics and, 3–4
  neutrality of, 29–30
  questions about conduct of, 55–63
  rationale for, 44–45
  real economy and, 4, 6, 55–56
  research on, 29–31
  set rule of, 55, 60–63, 93–94, 104–105
  shocks and, 46
  short-run effects of, 72
  simple models and, 58
  trial-and-error approach to, 4–5
  unemployment and, 10–11, 77, 104
  wishful thinking and, 77–78
Money supply, 3–4, 49–52, 72–73
Motley, Brian, 36

NAIRU. See Natural rate of unemployment

Natural rate of unemployment (NAIRU)
  in accelerationist model, 5
  changes in, 35–36
  increased, 11–12
  in long run, 91
  low, 77
  model, 24, 66
  Phillips Curve and, 82
  real wages and, 69
  uncertainty of, 14, 81–88, 91–92
  usage of term, 5
Neutral rate of unemployment
  in accelerationist model, 5, 9, 13
  central banks and, 11–12
  disinflation and, 11
  Eisner and, 18–19
  Gordon and, 17–18
  inflation and, 7
  labor market and, 6
  Phillips Curve and, 13–14
  Staiger et al.'s work and, 14
  uncertainty of, 13–15, 22
Nixon, Richard, 70
No long-run trade-off view, 29, 31–37

OECD countries, 11
Oil price shocks, 10–11, 40, 83
Okun's Law, 12, 38
Output stability, 38–41, 43–44, 47, 86–87
Owyong, Tuck Meng, 42–43

Penn-Central bankruptcy, 80
Phelps, Edmund S., 31, 35, 53–54
Phillips Curve
  accepted, 84, 103
  biases in econometric models of, 88
  Eisner's work and, 15–16, 18
  Gordon's work and, 13–14
  inflation and, 86

natural rate of unemployment and, 82
neutral rate of unemployment and, 13–14
non-existence of long-run trade-off and, 34–35
Staiger et al.'s work and, 23
standard accelerationist, 24
Point-for-point hypothesis, 35
Poole, William, 78–88, 91–93, 95–97
Pop economics, 4
Prescott, Edward, 44
Price index, 14
Price levels
  administered prices and, 2
  costs and, 2
  falling, 90
  in money equation, 49
  money supply and, 3–4
  oil, 10–11, 40, 83
  ratchet effect and, 2
  in recession, 1–2
  stability, 58, 74, 77
Price-setting institutions, 21
Price shocks, 40–41
Production possibilities curve, 38–41, 43–44
Productivity, 10, 36–37
Pushing on a string response to inflation, 23

Ratchet effect, 2
Rational expectations model of inflation, 33–34
Reagan, Ronald, 70
Real economy, 3–4, 6, 55–56, 59
Recession, 1–2, 74, 83–84, 90
Rutledge, John, 68

Sacrifice ratio, 21
Sargent, Thomas J., 35
Schultze, Charles, 2

Short-run trade-off view, 30, 37–44, 64
Social program cuts, 72
Solow, Robert M., 1–28, 55–59, 66, 68–69, 72, 76–80, 82–85, 87, 89–96, 100–101, 103–105
Staiger, Douglas, 14, 23
Stock, James, 14, 23
Stock market break (1987), 48
Supply-demand balance, 5, 12

Tax system, 72, 90
Taylor, John B., 29–64, 66, 68, 71–73, 78–82, 84–87, 94–101, 103–105
Taylor Rule, 94, 105
Thatcher, Margaret, 10
Time-inconsistency literature, 44–45, 62, 76
Tobin, James, 60

Unemployment. *See also* Natural rate of unemployment (NAIRU); Neutral rate of unemployment; Unemployment-inflation trade-off
accelerationist model and, 8–13
average level of, 63
in Canada, 8
central banks and, 17, 20
decreased, reasons for, 27–28
Eisner and, 17–19
in Europe, 8–10, 35–36
Federal Reserve and, 17, 85–86
Gordon and, 17–18
help-wanted index, 27
inflation and, 6–7, 37, 65, 85
job-vacancy rate and, 27
lagged, 23
monetary policy and, 10–11, 77, 104
pragmatism in discussion of, 4
in present times, 26

real economy and, 3
shock to rate of, 24
in United States, 8, 12, 32–33, 35–36
Unemployment-inflation trade-off
causal structure of, 103
evolution of intellectual foundations for, 53–54
interest rate rule and, 45–53
no long-run trade-off view, 29, 31–37
rationale for monetary policy and, 44–45
research on, 29–31
short-run trade-off view, 30, 37–44, 64
United Kingdom, 8–10
United States
Consumer Price Index and, 60
deficit reduction package of, 72
economy, 5–6, 54, 56
inflation in, 32–33
labor market in, 36
middle class in, 71
unemployment in, 8, 12, 32–33, 35–36
U.S. Bureau of Standards, 73–74

Variability trade-off, 38–44, 105
Volcker, Paul, 76–77

Wages
gap in, 10
nominal, 90
real, 10, 69
Wage-setting institutions, 21
Watson, Mark, 14, 23

Yellen, Janet, 98

Zero inflation rate, 31, 34, 66, 68, 74, 76, 90